Quiet in His Presence

Experiencing God's Love through Silent Prayer

Jan Harris

Baker Books
A Division of Baker Book House Co
Grand Rapids, Michigan 49516

© 2003 by Jan Harris

Published by Baker Books
a division of Baker Book House Company
P.O. Box 6287, Grand Rapids, MI 49516-6287
www.bakerbooks.com

Printed in the United States of America

ISBN 0-8010-6436-8

Library of Congress Cataloging-in-Publication Data if on file at the Library of Congress in Washington D.C.

To my parents, who gave their children one of life's greatest gifts—parents who loved each other unconditionally: darling Daddy, who loved me and gave himself for me and everyone he loved, modeling for me how God loves; dear Mum, whose enthusiasm for life and sense of adventure fueled my optimism about life

To Connie and David, Kelly and Rob, Michelle and Paul—may you always love and give yourselves for each other, and thereby carry on the family tradition

To Catherine

Contents

Part Three: How Being Quiet in His Presence Changes Your Life

Acknowledgments

I love the written word, especially when it is well written. And to me, well-written words are about listening. I grew up listening to the sound of well-written words—my parents read aloud to each other every evening: classics, children's books, the latest best-seller, poetry, whatever took their fancy.

In trying to put together some well-written words to explain my experience of God, I have listened to many kind, faithful, patient people, to whom I owe much gratitude.

Thanks to Baker Books' expert staff—Wendy, Karen, Stephanie—who have had to deal with an author who has been in publishing in one form or another far too long; to Mary Suggs, my painstaking and marvelous editor who cast herself in the role of reader and caught me every time I failed to explain what I meant; to Brian Peterson, whose dream of a world that knows God's love I share, and who reconnected with me at a crucial time; to the Torodes, the artists who created the cover, capturing the essence of my writing so perfectly.

Since 1990 a tiny handful of Australians have cheered me on, venturing with me into deeper and deeper waters of the Spirit, joyfully joining me as I led "basking in his presence" retreats. Thanks to mentor and alter ego Phyl Corben, who was outlining a book on centering prayer at the same time as I was but realized I was the one to write it; Phyl and her faithful little band supported me with prayers and by enthusiastically reading my early manuscript. Thanks to Pauline and her friends, and to others further afield.

Thanks to my family, friends, prayer group, and fellow parishioners at St. Barnabas's for taking an interest in the writing process, and for your love.

Thanks to many patient readers whose encouragement of and belief in me was vital: Jo Ann Carroll, Bill Clemmons, Dolores Milligan, Judy Schmidt, and Carl and Catharine Zelonis; to Joan Guest, an editor par excellence, whom I am lucky enough to have as a colleague and whose critique of my writing gave me hope. To Gary Bonikowsky and to Margaret Montreuil—each of you read, critiqued, and rewrote page after page, chapter after chapter, thoughtfully and carefully, always with humor and encouragement but with no strings attached.

Thanks to Jeannette Bakke, Jan Johnson, George Maloney, Mike Mason and Basil Pennington—all experienced contemplatives—for kindly reading my manuscript and even more kindly saying something good about it.

Thanks to two special people: Texas hermits Mary and Dennis. As full-time contemplatives living with joy in the Beloved, your eager willingness to read and comment on my manuscript in its early stages gave me the courage to begin the arduous process of submitting proposals to likely publishers. Blessings on you for seeing my book as a gift to seeking hearts and as a helpful addition to that which has been written by experts.

To my long-time colleague and mentor, Bill Volkman, whose untiring willingness to read aloud again—for it seems the hundredth time—every word, sentence, paragraph, page, and chapter, always honestly listening and catching the discordant phrase: more thanks and gratitude than I can ever express. I hope that this book will be a fitting companion for your marvelous book on centering prayer, published in 1996: *Basking in His Presence: A Call to the Prayer of Silence.*

Because the English language does not have gender-neutral pronouns, I have chosen to use the pronouns he, him, and his in the generic sense throughout my writing.

May what is true in all the words I have written linger in the hearts and minds like a sweet aroma, and may each reader catch a glimpse of God's goodness and their own belovedness.

Introduction

> It is a darkness of unknowing that lies between you and
> your God. . . . He whom [no one] . . . can grasp by knowl-
> edge can be *embraced by love.*
>
> From *The Cloud of Unknowing*

Have the glorious colors of a sunrise or a sunset ever
taken your breath away? Have you ever reached the
brow of a hill and been surprised by the unexpected
beauty of the landscape before you? Have you ever felt
at a loss for words in the midst of some wonder-filled
moment that has taken you by surprise? Filled with awe,
you become completely still while your heart feels as if
it will burst with the mystery and utter delight of this
overwhelming experience. You are immersed in the glow
of the present moment, transported briefly into a time-
less, trouble-free world—a world in which simply *being
there* is all that matters.

I can remember snippets of wonder-filled moments
from my very early childhood—praying and being aware
of God's presence all around me; sitting on the branch
of a peppercorn tree with my dad, looking up at the vast-
ness of the blue-black southern-hemisphere night sky
studded with glowing stars, and getting a sense of the

"bigness" of God; holding my mum's hand in a lamp-lit shed and wondering with her at the miracle of a tiny, newborn calf struggling to stand on the straw-strewn floor.

These moments defy explanation, because they are not a part of our ordinary, everyday life. Perhaps the only category we can safely put them in is that of a spiritual experience. Do such moments answer our questions about life, or do they merely engender more questions?

In 1990, after living most of my life as a Christian, I had a lot more questions about life and faith than I had answers. I was living in the Chicago area, attending an Episcopal church, and working for a Christian magazine based in the evangelical tradition. I'd had my share of wonder-filled moments, but my heart was still restless, longing for I knew not what. I wondered about prayer and, despite trying various methods, I had to admit that I really didn't know how I should pray. I longed for a dynamic reality in my spiritual life instead of what I was experiencing. I wanted a real, living, intimate relationship with God.

Pondering the lives of the saints of the past, especially the mystics, I found that a common thread appeared— a passionate love for God and a dimension of being in his presence that is rarely mentioned in contemporary Christian writings. In addition, many of them talked of God as if there was a dialogue going on between them. How could this be? I didn't understand how they had gotten to where they were. What did they know about a relationship with God that was still evading me? I wanted what they had!

Then, in the middle of that year, I stumbled across what was to be the most exciting discovery of my life. I came across the simple but ancient faith practice of contemplative prayer. This prayer changed my life. With its emphasis on being in God's presence *without words*, it was the culmination of a journey, a lifelong search.

Modern writers call contemplative prayer by a wide variety of names: the prayer of silence, centering prayer, the prayer of the heart, wordless prayer, listening prayer, the prayer of awareness, the prayer of unknowing, basking in his presence, inward prayer, meditation,[1] and so on. I use these terms interchangeably throughout the book. But it seems to me that above all else, the practice of contemplative prayer is an experience of God's love, hence my subtitle: *Experiencing God's Love through Silent Prayer*.

At about the same time as I discovered contemplative prayer, I opened a book that had been on my bookshelf unopened for a very long time. That book is *The Cloud of Unknowing*, written anonymously in England in the fourteenth century. It is an amazing book, the most exciting and inspiring that I have ever read, and it remains one that I turn to again and again. Reading it from cover to cover was so much easier than I had imagined, and when I was finished, I realized that it had changed my understanding of who God is and what he wants of us. The author tells us over and over again that the way to God is through *love* not knowledge: "It is a darkness of unknowing that lies between you and your God. . . . He whom [no one] . . . can grasp by knowledge can be *embraced by love*."[2]

I am still surprised that such an incredible guide to prayer, written so long ago, is virtually unread today! The unknown author, in his charmingly simple but profound style, speaks of God's presence being in a "dark *cloud of unknowing*."[3] Faith and trust in God's goodness toward us are paramount as we leave every known thing behind to seek God. This is how he puts it: "Just as the cloud of unknowing lies . . . between you and your God, so you must fashion a cloud of forgetting . . . between you and every created thing."[4]

We let go of all we know—all our *knowledge*—to humbly seek the One whom we want to know intimately through the *experience* of love. The author goes on: "When I speak of darkness, I mean the absence of knowledge. If you are unable to understand something . . . are you not in the dark as regards this thing? . . . It is a darkness of *unknowing* that lies between you and your God."[5] He says, "Learn to be at home in this darkness." He advises us of something that our knowledge-worshiping generation probably doesn't want to hear. During this life, we will remain in the dark about God. He says, "If, in this life, you hope to feel and see God as he is in himself, it must be within this *darkness* and this cloud."[6] This darkness is not a new idea. Paul says also that in this life "we see through a glass, *darkly*" (1 Cor. 13:12 KJV).

In contemporary society we worship knowledge—the false god that no one dares attack. It is our greatest obstacle to experiencing the Reality that is beyond our intellect. Until we get a taste of the contemplative wisdom that permeates that Reality, our mind and our ego are the only gods we know.

Adam and Eve chose to turn their backs on God to pursue knowledge. They chose to worship the false god of knowledge, instead of responding to the true God of love. We face the same choice. We can choose to pursue, through the intellect alone, knowledge about God; or we can respond to God and come to an intimate knowledge of him and his love through experience. The author of *The Cloud* warns us of the folly of idolizing knowledge. He wants us to understand that "no one can fully comprehend the uncreated God with his knowledge." He says that God created us in his image and likeness to love and worship him, the goal of our desire, and that it is "he alone who can fully satisfy the hunger and longing of our spirit." He continues, "He whom neither [we] nor angels can grasp by knowledge can be embraced by love."[7] Our loving God makes himself available to us through love.

The author of *The Cloud* also makes it clear that we are "drawn by *grace* to the contemplative work."[8] In other words, we are drawn or called *by God* to the prayer of love, to silent prayer—the prayer of unknowing. We do not choose ourselves; we are chosen. Our part is always to respond.

One of the main reasons I find *The Cloud* so exciting and inspiring is because the author speaks so eloquently about a God of *love*. My heart sings when I read what he writes about a God whose love for us "is so great that his heart could not rest satisfied" till he "awakened desire" within us and drew us "closer to himself."[9]

My own experience of God is of a gentle and patient lover who woos his beloved into his arms. I rejoice in the author's insistence that "He whom [no one] . . . can grasp by knowledge *can* be embraced by love." That means that the simple, the ordinary, and the uneducated—in other words, most of the world's population—can have a relationship with this marvelous God for whom love is *all*. No one is left out; everyone can approach God, for we all come clothed, not in knowledge but in love.

To me contemplative prayer is a lot like making love. It is uniquely personal to each of us, and it is best to leave the technique up to the lovers. Even though this is true, I needed a little help to get started, and perhaps you do too. Chapter 6, "Steps to Being Quiet in His Presence," is for those who need some simple suggestions on how to do this prayer. Once we begin, we can trust the Lord to lead us. Then, like the steps of two dancers whose hearts are in tune with each other and with the music, prayer becomes a dance with our beloved Lord in harmonious, spontaneous, and unself-conscious abandon.

As our hearts gradually get in tune with the Lord in the silence, he takes our burdens on himself, lightening our load, and setting us free. We will find ourselves embarking on a healing journey as we surrender ourselves to his infinite love.

I am not an expert on contemplative prayer—I am a beginner. I am an Anglican for whom faith is a private matter, and I usually share it only when asked. But my heart aches when I meet people, both inside and outside the church, who are searching for God. They don't know how to find him, and yet, for those who truly seek him with their whole heart, he is so easily found!

I am not a priest, pastor, or Bible teacher. I have had no theological or philosophical training. This book, therefore, is not a theological or philosophical argument for adding the practice of contemplative prayer to one's devotional life. It is merely the account of my experience as a person in love with and loved by God. It is an invitation to all who read it to step away for a moment from all the words we make up to say to God, into the silence of God's presence. It is an invitation to step into the stream of love that flows continuously between God the Father and Jesus the Son through the power of the Holy Spirit.

Some aspects of my life journey have been traumatic. I share them with some trepidation, not to shock you but to demonstrate how contemplative prayer—the prayer of love—has ministered to me. It is not just for the superreligious or supergood. It is a prayer for us all.

It is also a prayer for God—because in it we give ourselves as a gift to him. We come empty-handed, silent, childlike. The Lord accepts us and rejoices over us with great joy.

God loves us passionately and unconditionally. He delights in us. He sings love songs to us. He has filled his world with love notes written to us, his beloved—beautiful flowers, glorious sunsets, pink and gold sunrises, brilliantly blue night skies filled with glittering stars, the sounds of birdsong, rippling streams, and beautiful music.

Are we missing out on what God wants to say to us? Are we so busy that we don't have time to listen to the words of love that fill the universe? God calls on us to respond, to turn to him, and to give ourselves to him without reservation, so that he can set us free from the chains that bind us.

To all who ponder God's infinite love and are longing to respond to him, I encourage you to make a date with your Beloved and be prepared to give yourself as a gift to him. Once or twice a day, give the Lord fifteen to twenty minutes (or even five minutes) and just be still and quiet in his presence.

I speak to myself when I say, Don't let anything get in your way. Set aside time every day for the prayer of silence. Accept that you are the Lord's beloved. Find time for him. And get ready to enjoy the most delightful part of your day!

Part I

Why Be . . .
Quiet in His Presence?

Giving yourself up to love is melting into God. It is falling
into the hands of the living God with complete abandon. This is the deep interior prayer for which we have
been striving. Here we must let go of our dependency
on thoughts, words, and images. We go into the beautiful darkness. We stop struggling. We let the angels
carry us. Surrender is the only word we know. We let go
even of our yearning for God. Nothing is left except
being in God. What could I say that would matter when
I am in the heart of God? Beautiful darkness! Contemplation! All words are digested. Contemplation is like
going to heaven for a while.

Macrina Wiederkehr
A Tree Full of Angels

I

A Particular Love

For we do not know *how* we ought to pray; the Spirit himself pleads with God for us in groans that words cannot express.

Romans 8:26 GNB

It was time for the retreat weekend in Dallas to come to a close. Throughout the day and a half, the retreatants had been encouraged to see themselves as God's special people; to give themselves to him as gifts; to see themselves as precious, the beloved children of the Father, as bride to the Bridegroom; and to surrender themselves to the mystery of God's love. They had been led gently into "the cloud of unknowing" and had begun to trust God to love them into wholeness. They had been urged to rest in the Lord, to come to him as a weaned child— with no agenda—and to accept his unconditional love. They had come, opened themselves to his love, and had been immersed in the communal practice of centering prayer. Sitting in silence for twenty minutes, these seek-

19

ers—many of them first-time retreatants—were amazed at how quickly those twenty minutes passed.

Just before the final prayer, as they sat in a circle, each participant was given as much time as needed to share what was on his or her heart.

One woman hesitantly began speaking: "Before this, I'd never thought about how much God loves me. I guess I just never really thought it mattered. I loved him and I wanted to do things for him. If I did, then I knew he would be pleased. But to have him *want* to be with me—and me alone—I'd never thought about that before.

"As I sat here in the silence, I began to accept that it was true that the Lord wanted to be with *me*—and I gradually saw things differently.

"I was one of six children. Growing up, I knew that my parents loved me, but I didn't feel that they loved me *particularly*.

"When I grew up, I became a missionary. I knew that God loved me, but I didn't feel that he loved me *particularly*." As she spoke, her face began to glow. "Now I know that he loves me *particularly*."

In this book I want to share with you the mystery of God's love for us, and why I state unequivocally that he loves us *passionately* and *particularly*. When we give up all we know and trust God to love us into wholeness, we will discover that not only does God love us passionately and particularly, but, paradoxically, each one of us is specially and uniquely his one and only love. In other words, the Lord loves each one of us as if each were the only person in the world. He made us for love, and he is calling each individual one of us into his loving presence, into the mystery of unknowing, into the prayer of silence.

The story is told of a priest who went to visit Ireland. One evening, as he walked along a country road, he came across an old man also out enjoying the twilight air. They walked and talked together until a sudden rain made them take shelter. When their conversation moved into silence, the old man took out a prayer book and began praying quietly to himself.

The priest watched him for a long while. Then in a quiet whisper he said, "You must be very close to God!"

The old man smiled and answered, "Oh, aye! The Father is very fond of me!"[1]

God is very fond of you! And he's very fond of me! And, just like that old Irishman who knew the Lord was very fond of him, we can know for sure too.

Romans 8:26 says, "For we do not know *how* we ought to pray" (GNB). We are told to "pray without ceasing" (1 Thess. 5:17), and yet, when it comes right down to it, we scarcely know *how* to pray. We frail human creatures find that prayer, loving God, and living a spiritual life all have a mysterious quality to them. No matter how much we want to, we don't know *how* to do any of these things. Yet, the fact is, because our lives are "hidden with Christ in God" (Col. 3:3), *we* are prayer.

Jesus lived a life of "unknowing." When he came to live among us, there were, no doubt, a lot of things about being human that he had to learn by experience. He had to live "by faith, not by sight" (2 Cor. 5:7). Even though he is "true God from true God,"[2] Jesus gave it all up— emptying himself for love's sake—to step into a cloud of unknowing for us. Even though he had something we don't have—an abiding awareness of his loving Father— he took time to nurture his relationship with him. Jesus knew that he needed to be alone with the Father, to love and be loved, because he was totally dependent on his Father's love.

We too are totally dependent on our Father's love. We see this when we come to God in silence and enter into the cloud of unknowing. Casting ourselves totally into

21

God's arms, coming quietly into his presence, we open our hearts to his healing touch. We open our ears to hear his gentle whispers of love. We begin to believe that we are truly loved, cherished, and precious to the Beloved, who is calling us into the mystery of love—into an intimate relationship with himself.

Once we admit that Paul is right and that we really don't know how to pray, then we can clear the decks and begin from the beginning. We come like baby birds, with our mouths open, waiting for the Lord to feed us; we come like beggars, with our hands cupped, ready to receive the gifts the Lord has for us, ready to become prayer.

I struggled for years trying to figure out *how* to pray, not realizing that the *how* of prayer had to become the *who* of prayer. Who am I? I am the Lord's beloved. He's very fond of me! He wants me to seek him out and just be with him for himself.

For as long as I can remember, I've wanted a close and intimate relationship with the Lord. There were years when I thought that's what I had. Being a very optimistic Pollyanna-type, my prayers were mostly adoration for and praise to a God who created a beautiful world filled with things to enjoy. I learned to pray simple prayers about my needs or those of others, but I've never been much good at long intercessory prayers. Even in the midst of tragedy, my prayers were much more a few words of praise than many words of petition. Talking or writing, I had plenty of words; when it came to prayer, I had very little to say.

Years into my faith journey, I realized that, apparently, my prayer practice was different from that of other Christians. I assumed my way of doing it was wrong, so when someone spoke about prayer, I listened carefully and then tried what had been suggested. I would try it for a while, but it just didn't feel right to me. I couldn't quite figure out how to make prayer work the way the teachers said it should. I wondered what the secret was.

When I discovered contemplative prayer—the prayer of silence—it felt right. Just being with God in silence seemed to be what I had been looking for all along. I could come empty-handed and without words to God, give myself to him as a gift, worship and adore him for himself, and accept that he *wanted* to be with me. This prayer was for me!

Admitting that I didn't know how I ought to pray was a great relief. I suspect that this is true for us all. Once we realize that we don't know how to pray, we free the Holy Spirit to guide us into contemplative prayer—the *prayer of unknowing*. Intellectually knowing about or having an interest in silent prayer without actually practicing it cannot give us the transforming experience of God's all-encompassing love that changes our lives. Only immersing ourselves in the silence, for God's sake, can.

When Paul says, "For we do not know how we ought to pray; the Spirit himself pleads with God for us in groans that words cannot express" (Rom. 8:26 GNB), is he speaking the truth or is he exaggerating? Does God need *advice* from us on how to fix our problems? Or can we, without saying a word, trust the Holy Spirit to communicate with God so that our heart's longings and desires are made known? Beloved children do not have to tell their parents their needs and wants; their parents have already anticipated them long before the children have even thought of them. Knowing our heart, God anticipates our needs and desires.

The truth that we are beloved, cherished, and precious to God sounds wonderful, but it is a concept that is hard for most of us to believe, so we must *practice* believing it. We listen to the words—*beloved* and *cherished* and *precious*—repeat them to ourselves, meditate on them, and then take the truth of them with us into

23

the silence of the prayer of the cloud of unknowing. Being aware of God in this way, we are gradually healed from our wounds of unlove, and we are able to say, "God is crazy about me. He loves me unconditionally."

The desire of God's heart is for each of us to know that we are the apple of his eye and that he loves each one of us passionately and particularly. Silent contemplative prayer takes us directly to God's heart and leaves us there in his arms—where we entrust ourselves to him and bask in his presence.

If you want to "love God more dearly"[3] and know without a doubt that he loves you too, then I encourage you to take a few minutes each day to sit with him in silence and give God a chance to reveal to you how particularly he loves you.

2

Drawn by Love's Longing

The eternal love of God . . . could not bear to let you go on living so common a life far from him. And so, with exquisite kindness, he awakened desire within you, and binding it fast with *the leash of love's longing,* drew you closer to himself . . .

From *The Cloud of Unknowing*

My childhood was spent on my parents' farm in the fertile southeast of Australia, in Victoria, not far from Melbourne, the state capital. Farms there are small (one thousand acres or less). In addition to his Merino sheep, which were bred for their fine wool, my dad had beef and dairy cattle, as well as horses, dogs, ducks, geese, and hens.

Like most Aussie sheep farmers, my dad had carefully bred and trained dogs to help him with his flock of sheep. Each year Lassie (yes, we have Lassies in Australia too!), our longhaired, brown and white Border collie, gave birth to a litter of nine puppies.

Our whole family watched closely those nine adorable balls of fluff. We waited for the day when their legs would be long enough to lift their fat tummies off the ground and steady enough to wobble around. That's when their training to be working dogs would begin.

The first thing my father taught them was to come to him. He would put a collar on a reluctant puppy, attach a leash to the collar, and then, talking softly, he would slowly draw the unwilling puppy toward him.

The puppy would alternately shake his head, trying to dislodge the collar, dig his heels in, growl, howl, and then move forward a few steps. Eventually the leash would draw him to the source of the soft voice speaking to him—and my father's outstretched hand. The hand would begin to stroke his head and fondle his ears. The puppy's body would relax. After a moment he would roll over on his back, exposing his bare pink belly to my dad's fondling hand. The puppy's head would loll to one side, and he would relinquish himself to the newfound pleasure of being in his master's presence.

Border collies quickly learn to adore their masters— and they love to work for them. Properly trained, they become extensions of their master, learning to anticipate his every whim, as well as every move of the sheep in the flock. One of Dad's dogs, Bobby, was completely in tune with him. No matter how closely we watched my dad, we rarely could keep up with his instructions, but Bobby could. We would watch Dad's lips, hands, and head for the slightest movement, but apart from an occasional whistle command, we saw and heard nothing. Bobby, however, worked the sheep, a big "grin" on his doggy face, and one eye fixed on my dad the whole time!

Just like the Border collie puppies, we are being drawn to fulfill our destiny. We are being drawn toward a love relationship with God, toward being *extensions* of him.

"The eternal love of God . . . could not bear to let you go on living so common a life far from him. And so, with exquisite kindness, he awakened desire within you, and binding it fast with *the leash of love's longing,* drew you closer to himself."[1] When we move toward God, we are not fully aware that our destiny is all about love. God draws us to himself to *love* us into wholeness. He wants to give himself to us, to have mercy on us, to give us his peace, and to bring us to a place where we will rest in him. God, who loves each one of us particularly, longs to share his life with us and have an intimate relationship with us. So he awakens desire in us for that relationship and draws us closer to himself.

We were made to hunger and thirst for love and fulfillment, but we don't always recognize what it is we want. The woman at the well had lived her whole life trying to find it. When Jesus spoke kindly and truthfully to her, she realized in a flash that *he* was the object of her desire—and she quickly and boldly acknowledged her need. We can do the same.

When we become aware of our longing for God and respond to his drawing us, we will find the Lover of our souls is already waiting for us. We draw close to him through the prayer of adoration and silence, we give ourselves to God in love, we accept that he loves us, and we surrender to his warm embrace. As we rest in him, we notice that he is whispering reassuring words to us and is touching our hearts with his tender love.

One of the most difficult periods of my life came just as I was beginning to be comfortable with the practice and sharing of the prayer of silence. In January 1993 my beloved dad was diagnosed with Alzheimer's disease. Even before the diagnosis, my mum had had trouble accepting the truth of what was happening. She struggled to cover up for Dad, and she alone became his protector, caretaker, and nurse. By October my mother was exhausted. Her wise gerontologist realized that her health was deteriorating faster than my dad's.

The obvious answer was to get help for Mum. We all breathed a sigh of relief when we found a small aged-care hostel just a short drive from my brother's house. Run by caring people, the hostel treated everyone like part of the family, and a personal-care nurse was available to help Mum with my dad if needed. In December 1993 my parents moved into a double room and gradually settled into the hostel routine. They began to get used to the help that was provided and started getting to know the other thirty residents.

Very early one morning of the following March, we were shocked to learn that a fire had raged through the hostel during the night, and my mother was one of four who had died from smoke inhalation. My heartbroken brother, who had been awakened with the news, called me shortly afterward. I immediately flew back to Australia and spent the next few months there.

My dad survived, suffering for months from the effects of the smoke. He and other residents were housed in hospitals nearby until they recovered and the hostel was rebuilt. The shock accelerated the progression of Dad's Alzheimer's, so we never did figure out to what extent he was aware of Mum's death. After the fire, he spent more and more of his time living way back in the past.

I found it almost impossible to come to terms with the shock and pain of this family tragedy. Life had an unreal quality to it, and I found it very difficult to concentrate on anything. In hindsight it seems to me that in all the heartbroken tears that were shed, in the many nights when sleep wouldn't come, in dealing with autopsy reports, police, fire brigade, and arson investigations, we as a family were "helping to complete what still remains of Christ's sufferings" (Col. 1:24 GNB).

There was no question in my mind that God's love surrounded and sustained us all during this time, as we visited my dad in the hospital daily while he recovered, as we planned the funeral, and as we consoled and were consoled by the love, tears, and prayers of shocked extended family and friends. A sudden, tragic death is not something to be "gotten over with" as soon as possible. In the week between my mother's death and her funeral, my brother and I talked about the time that we all needed to grieve, to mourn, and to heal.

We carefully planned the funeral service, choosing familiar, comforting prayers, Bible readings, and favorite hymns. Shortly before my mum died, I had discovered a wonderful tape by a Celtic musician. A poem written by Clare of Assisi to her sister Agnes had been put to music in a hauntingly beautiful song of farewell, which we played at the service. A few of the words are:

> After all the words,
> What more can I say?
> The love which I have for you, my friend,
> Glows ever sweetly in my heart.
> When you come before the Lord,
> Remember my name,
> And know I've inscribed in my soul
> The happy memory of your love.
>
> But before I say farewell,
> There is one thing I must add,
> That you cling with all your heart,
> To the One who is our life,
> Whose love inflames our love,
> Whose beauty all admire,
> Whose gentleness is peace,
> Our gracious Lord.[2]

The phrases "After all the words, what more can I say?" and "The happy memory of your love" specially touched me at the time and still do. "Cling with all your heart to the One who is our life . . . our gracious Lord" was particularly comforting. I found, over the next few months, that this was all I could do—I clung with all my heart to the Lord, my life. The only way I could deal with the numbing pain of this awful tragedy was to draw close to God and tuck myself into his loving arms.

I was completely beyond words. I couldn't pray verbally. An abbreviated version of the Jesus prayer—"Lord, have mercy"—was all I ever uttered. *The Cloud of Unknowing* says, "You must abandon them all [all things—whether material or spiritual] beneath the cloud of forgetting,"[3] and "let your longing [for God] relentlessly beat upon the cloud of unknowing that lies between you and your God."[4] And that is what I had to do. I abandoned myself to the prayer of unknowing, because I had no idea how to pray. The raw pain made me aware of God's loving nudges and made me much less impatient with other people's needs and their pain.

After returning to the United States, I found that I needed a lot of time alone—working in the garden, walking in the park, or just *being,* mostly in silence. A few of my friends understood. Some did not. I was healing. My loved ones were healing. And my awareness of the gentleness, goodness, and kindness of God became more acute with each passing day. As I read poems and writings by saints from the past, I found that most of them echoed what I was experiencing of God's love—a love that inflamed my love.

From the beginning of my discovery of the prayer of silence, I had shared it with others in retreats. At each retreat I led, I watched the healing balm of God's presence become a reality as we novices sat together in silence in his name, practicing his presence.

30

Sitting together with others in silence in the presence of the Lord, I found that two pictures frequently came to my mind. One was of a small, trusting child finding nurture, comfort, and love in the arms of a parent; and the other was of a bride being called to intimacy by the bridegroom.

The image of bride and bridegroom—of lovers—is the central feature of the Song of Songs. The conventional interpretation of this seldom-read book is nice and safe. It's an allegory of the relationship between Christ and the church, the body of Christ. What if it's actually closer to home than that? Could it be that Christ, the Bridegroom, is speaking to each individual person who makes up his body? Could it be that the love and intimacy portrayed here is God's intention for each one of us? Does he intend for us to stay hidden in the corporate body, or is he calling us by name individually into an intimate relationship with himself?

The author of *The Cloud* says, "The eternal love of God . . . could not bear to let you go on living so . . . far from him." Imagine—the Lord could not bear it! So, "he awakened desire within you, and . . . drew you closer to himself." Has God awakened desire in you? Don't you long for the passionate, loving embrace of the Bridegroom? Shouldn't this be the heart's desire of a bride? Yet it seems that both the world and the church are so busy with other things that they keep the bride from hearing the call from her Lover.

The author of *The Cloud* ponders the wonder of God's all-encompassing love for us:

> Truly this is the unending miracle of love: that one loving person, through his love, can embrace God, whose being fills and transcends the entire creation . . . to experience this love is the joy of eternal life. . . . Now do you see why I raise you to this spiritual work? You would

have taken to it naturally had [we] not sinned, for [we were] created to make love possible. Nevertheless, by the work of contemplative love [we] will be healed.[5]

This is the miracle! That one loving person can embrace God and can be embraced by him! This is how we live eternal life now—through the work of contemplative love. In the silence we are healed of the wounds sin has inflicted.

Each human being is made in God's image and therefore longs to be loved. Yet it is often only through the pain of personal tragedy and emotional turmoil that we become aware of that longing and our desire for wholeness and meaning.

God, with exquisite kindness, draws us, one reluctant step after another, to him, so that we can finally give our whole self to the newfound joy of just being in his loving arms. He cannot bear that we live so far from him. He longs for us to trust ourselves to him, to immerse ourselves in the cloud of unknowing, to cling to him with all our hearts, and to give ourselves up to the wonder of his eternal love.

3

Made for Love

Our hearts are made for you, Lord.

St. Augustine

It was a cool, damp morning in Snowdonia, Wales. I took the tourist train and got out at the station halfway up Mount Snowdon. Walking down the hill a little, away from the train station and the people, I came to a rock, half-buried in purple heather.

As I sat there, completely alone, with the sun shining weakly behind me and the valley below shrouded in mist, my head was filled with whirling thoughts. I began questioning God again about what he was doing in my life. Suddenly I was walking on a slippery downhill slope through a dark tunnel, and there was no end in sight.

Darkness descended on me, and walking became scary. I wasn't sure where to put my feet. With every faltering step I was more and more aware of the slick path underfoot. I couldn't see my way ahead. I couldn't even see my hand in front of my face. And I was cold.

I put out my hands on either side of me, feeling for the guardrail that had always been there; my arms flailed empty air. There was no guardrail! How could I possibly walk without it? Now I was really scared.

I closed my eyes, realizing that the darkness was no greater even with my eyes closed. Opening them again, I hoped that the darkness would have gone. But it was just as dark. I stood completely still. I couldn't possibly go on, but neither could I turn back.

"Oh, God! Where are you? What's happening?" I whimpered.

Then, as I stood there, motionless, I became aware of a calmness overtaking me.

I'm here.

I stayed completely still, aware only of my breathing and the overwhelming assurance that I was not alone.

You can walk safely.

"But I can't see!"

You don't need to see. I won't let you fall.

"But I've never walked without the guardrail before."

Just trust me. You'll be fine.

Very cautiously, I took a step. The path was still slippery. I still couldn't see a thing in front of me. But I didn't fall, and I wasn't scared anymore, just aware that I was on an unfamiliar path and that I had to walk it by faith not sight.

I looked down at my feet and realized they were firmly planted on the ground, in the heather that surrounded the rock on which I was sitting. The sun was shining brightly now, and the mist in the valley had cleared.

I stood up and walked back to the train station, mulling over what I had just experienced. Whether it was a vision or a daydream, all I knew was that it had answered a lot of my questions about what was going on in my life.

34

The year was 1976. Since 1960 I had been a member of a legalistic religious group (cult?) for whom everything was spelled out. The leaders of the group determined what righteousness was, and we followers willingly (in most cases) tried to obey them. There was a rule for everything you can imagine. Many of the rules were very good ones, taken straight from the more than six hundred rules given to the Jews in the first five books of the Bible.

My first adult experience of church had been with this group. In the early '60s, with the threat of nuclear war hanging over my dreams for the future, I was introduced to Bible prophecy. Scared, I read everything I could lay my hands on, eagerly reading the Bible, as the Bereans did, "to see whether these things were so" (Acts 17:11).

During my growing-up years, my parents set an example of quiet, loving trust in God and nurtured a freedom to question, to think, and to test everything. From early childhood, I had known Jesus as my friend. As an Anglican, at confirmation, I had learned the Ten Commandments and the creeds. But I had never heard about prophecy, about the myriad laws of Moses, nor the commands about Sabbaths and feast days. So I took my new study seriously, spending many hours daily and going to the public library. My entire lifestyle changed, as I tried to incorporate into my life as many as possible of the Levitical laws.

Saturday became a day of complete rest from any physical or secular activities. My husband finished work at three o'clock on Friday afternoon, and all shopping and food preparation were completed before the sun went down. Then we would have our candlelit dinner, beginning a twenty-four-hour period of prayer, Bible study, and meditation. (At one point, we went so far as to eat only cold food and leave the beds unmade.)

Seven special feast days throughout the year were observed in the same way as the weekly Sabbath. I was challenged to learn as much as I could about this yearly cycle of religious observances, and I was anxious to settle into a routine.

This religious group considered themselves the one true church, and all others were false, either not true Christians or downright pagan and evil. The rules were clear. Certain foods were off-limits. Labels on all foods were carefully read, and I became a loyal customer of the local health food store. Certain fabrics were forbidden. Reading anything apart from that which was produced or recommended by the group was forbidden, with the exception of reputable newspapers and newsmagazines. Though an avid reader as a child and young adult, during those years I did not read a single novel. Movies, plays, and TV programs were considered time wasters. The only movies I can remember seeing during that time were *The Sound of Music, The Ten Commandments,* and *Ben Hur.* Pop music was out. Most secular holidays, birthdays, and all religious observances, including Christmas and Easter, were forbidden.

After about three years, we moved to an area in which many others in the same group lived, and we became very involved in an active social life. Friendships outside the group (as well as relationships with family members who were not part of the church) were not encouraged; life became very safe and predictable.

Once I settled into the routine of trying to obey the rules, attend church, and ask the leaders' advice on every decision in life, I became bored and restless. I had grown up in a household in which we had been encouraged to think; so, halfway through our fourth year as a part of this group, I began to think about what I was doing. I started questioning everything. Shortly after that my husband died in a car crash and, afraid that I had angered

God, my questioning stopped. As I struggled to survive, my questions lay buried. Only occasionally would I allow a tentative question to surface in my private prayer time.

I moved to the next state to work at the church's international office. And I began dating. Dating was required for all singles, as marriage within the group was encouraged. So life became very busy. I moved overseas and, after a number of years, I remarried. Soon the questions began again. This time I wasn't the only one asking them. I had a few friends who would also occasionally raise a question.

Early in 1975 I began to wonder again about the church. *Why don't we love each other the way Jesus said his followers would?* I had to admit to myself that the most loving people in our group did not have anywhere near the quality of love Paul speaks about in 1 Corinthians 13. It was obvious that there was more to love than keeping the laws we had all been trying to keep all these years. I could look back and see that obeying the church laws was getting no easier, and neither my friends nor I were any nearer the perfection for which we were all striving. I could see that we all knew a lot about the Bible and the laws but, I asked myself, *Does this mean we are any closer to the heart of the Lawgiver?* Either God was asking for the impossible, or he had some other answer that we were missing.

In my frustration, I asked God to show me his love. Then I began randomly reading the Bible, in much the same openhearted way I had read it in 1960. I was astonished at what I read! The biggest shock came from reading Galatians. This book had been our "proof text" for the meticulous keeping of all of the Levitical laws. A friend called me and said, "Just pretend that you have never read the Bible before. Now read the entire Book of Galatians, and then tell me what it says."

When I had read it all the way through, I shared my discovery with my husband. Then I called my friend and said, "We're wrong! We've been wrong all along! We're just like the Galatians! This book says *not* to keep all those laws that we've been trying to keep. No wonder we can't love like Paul says in 1 Corinthians 13!"

The next Saturday, during my early morning walk through the woods, I took a detour. On my way home, even though it was a scary thing to do, I went to the store. I had never been in a store on a Saturday before. I bought a small item (which I didn't really need). Nothing happened. The sky didn't fall in on me. That afternoon, for the first time, I sat in church and listened critically to the sermon. I also began to wonder if other churches were *really* evil. The next time I went shopping, I bought some "forbidden food."

I kept reading the Bible, and I began to notice a strange thing. It seemed that every chapter I read had the same message as Galatians. Finally, it dawned on me that the entire religious system we were dedicated to was wrong! If the entire system I had been following was wrong, then I didn't need to keep any of the Sabbaths, feast days, food or clothing laws! My mind boggled. My nice, safe world was beginning to come apart.

It was at that point that we began to share our discovery with our friends. Some listened and agreed. Some listened and reported us to the leadership. Some people got very angry. Some people remained friends. Some ostracized us. The leaders decided that excommunication was their only recourse.

I went to pick up my things from my office, and everything was gone. They had already cleaned it out. When I went shopping later that day, some of our friends walked out of the shop when I walked in. Others saw me coming along the street and crossed to the other side to avoid me.

It felt really strange, and I was puzzled. In many ways, I was still the same person. Suddenly, my world had completely changed, and I was dazed and a little bewildered. All I had done was ask God to reveal to me what love is. And he had. He showed me that love isn't just obeying the rules. When I shared this with people, it scared them. Most of my friends deserted me, and I felt very much alone.

I couldn't remember ever walking alone with God. For fifteen years I had had the security of all of those rules, of my friends, and of the pastor and leaders telling me what to do and what to think. Suddenly I had no job and very few friends. More than half the population of the small English village I lived in belonged to the religious group that had ostracized me. I knew no one outside the group.

Then, unexpectedly, some people from the group began to turn up at our home to talk. It soon became a constant stream, with some coming late at night and others before dawn to avoid being seen. Some walked through the woods at the back of the house and came in the back door. When I noticed an unfamiliar van had been parked across the narrow street for several days, I realized that the house was being watched night and day to see who was visiting. On one of my daily walks I boldly peered in the passenger-side window, and I surprised the occupant, who had a movie camera trained on the house!

If one does not obey all the laws given to Israel, I wondered, *how does one please God?* Around and around in my head went the questions: *What is the answer? What does the Bible really say?*

The answer kept coming back: *Follow me!*

But what am I to do? Am I being deceived? Is this the way of the God of love?

The answer kept coming back: *You're not deceived. I am Love.*

To get time to think, to get away from the stream of people, and to catch up on sleep, my husband and I had gone to a quiet cottage at the foot of Mount Snowdon, in nearby Wales. For the first couple of days I just slept late, escaped by reading some novels I had bought at Kings Cross station in London, or walked up and down the mountain.

One morning I took the tourist train, and when it stopped at the station halfway up the mountain, I got out. That was when I sat alone on a rock, and God showed me that I was not walking alone but that he was with me in this numbing darkness. The guardrails that I had been looking for were the rules and the people that I had come to rely on instead of relying on God. The time had come for them all to go. It was time for me to see my loving God as all I needed to survive.

It was during that time that I first became aware that the Lord was not separate from me. I could not see in the dark, but he could. I did not know where the path through the darkness was going, but he did. And just as he promised, he was with me. I learned to let go of my reliance on externals and put my trust in him. I learned that God loved me and was with me in the darkness.

Over the next few months there were many times when I was tempted to go back to the group, tell them that I had been wrong, and beg them to let me come back to the safety of the spelled-out rules. As soon as I would consider it, I would be overwhelmed by God's warm and comforting presence. It was as if he took my hand on that slippery, downhill path in the darkness and reassured me that I didn't need to be afraid.

After about eighteen months, the darkness began to give way to light. One day I noticed that the birds were singing. Then I realized that the sun was shining, and the flowers were blooming. I was delighted to see how brightly the sunlight shone through the leaves in the late afternoon sun.

I missed church, but I was afraid to walk into a strange one and find that I was expected to learn and obey a new set of rules. I dared to listen carefully to church services on the radio and then on television. One day in the summer, while out shopping, I walked into a fourteenth-century Anglican church at noon with a bunch of tourists and accepted an invitation to stay for the short service that was just beginning. It seems bizarre now, but as I sat there, I kept looking at the ancient stone walls and wondering if they would fall in on me! To my relief, they didn't, nor did I get struck by lightning when I walked out! I was surprised to hear people in that church talking about God as if they knew him.

I persuaded my husband to come with me to that same church the following Sunday evening. During the service, I was filled with wonder and awe as wave after wave of warmth and love swept over me when the entire congregation of at least a thousand sang gently in the Spirit. To me, it was as if angels were leading the worship! This experience, plus the diversity in age and social status of the people, the subdued exuberance and enthusiasm in the packed church, the short, simple, but sound explanation of the Scripture readings, and the sincere interest of the members in visitors, convinced me that God was truly in this place.

The gentle love of Jesus for his people that enveloped me during those services captured my heart, and I could see that I didn't need to be afraid. I hadn't "accidentally" walked into that church. The Lord, who had been with me in the scary darkness, was still showing me the path on which to walk. Over the next several months, as I became a part of the congregation, I fell deeply in love with the Lord.

I had known a lot about dos and don'ts, rules and laws, but I hadn't known about the love of Jesus. Reading the Gospels and the Epistles had caused me to question, "Where is the love Jesus speaks about?" Now, I had discovered it.

My journey over the next decade was to include a healing of the rift between my Anglican beginnings and my subsequent religious experience, my embracing of both the charismatic and the eucharistic, an abiding awareness of my union with Christ, and eventually a coming to rest in him in the silence of contemplative prayer.

The tender love that I discovered Jesus had for me, he has for everyone. This is why he came—to share this love with us. Our hearts are made for love, and when we feel that longing for love, we assume that we will be able to get it from another human being. So, early in our lives, we set out on our search for love, sure that what we find will be perfect. We long for our heart to be touched, to swell with love until it seems to be bursting. We dream about finding that one special person who will love us unconditionally, adore us, cherish us, give all for us. We expect to be able to return that love. To love unconditionally and to be loved in return is the cry of the human heart.

After we find our special person, sooner or later we have to admit that deep down inside of us there is still an emptiness, a vague sense of loneliness, of unfulfillment, of dissatisfaction, a feeling that something is missing. Why? Because *no human being can fulfill all of our needs*. It's expecting too much of a mere mortal. Only God can fill the emptiness. He made us in his image so that only he can answer the deepest cry of the human heart. Only when our spirit is one with the Spirit of

Christ—in a loving union—will our heart's cry be answered.

After the experience of Pentecost, when their hearts were filled with the Holy Spirit, Jesus' first-century followers began to understand the meaning of "For God so loved the world that He gave" (John 3:16). They were so touched by his love for them that they couldn't contain themselves. They rushed out and related the gospel to everyone they met, eager to share the gift of love that had been bestowed on them. They realized that (as the angel proclaimed to Mary) this was the good news for *all* people, not a secret for them to keep to themselves. They had found what their hearts were made for. They had found their loving Lord.

But what about us? Have we found what our hearts were made for? Our hearts were made to respond to love. A tiny baby, as soon as he becomes aware that he is loved, begins to return that love. As St. Augustine said, "Our hearts are made for you, Lord."[1] The One who loved us first calls us to respond.

The Lord longs for us to drop our busyness for a moment and simply loll in his lap in adoration and wordless communion. Let's accept the fact that we who felt we were the unloved have *always* been his beloved; we who felt abandoned were never forsaken. Let's allow our hearts to be touched, and let's return his love. Like little children who are sure of their welcome, let's run boldly to our God, fling ourselves into his arms, and surrender to his love.

4

"In All Things . . ."

In all things God works for the good of those who love
him.

Romans 8:28 NIV

It was 6 P.M. and I was exhausted. I'd worked my normal day—most of it spent juggling the various responsibilities as office manager of a Christian magazine. I
called my husband as I was leaving the office, telling
him that I would be stopping at the grocery store on my
way home. I was looking forward to a quiet evening.

It was just before 7 P.M. when I pulled the car into the
garage, dragged my groceries into the kitchen, and
started up the stairs to my husband's office. He met me
halfway, with a scowl on his face.

"Where have you been? Why did it take you so long?
What time do you expect to serve dinner?" he shouted.

Dismayed, I backed down the stairs, with him following me. As I reached the last couple of steps, he gave
me a shove, and I landed in a heap at the bottom of the
carpeted stairs.

"Did you get the artichoke hearts for the salad?"

Darn! He'd told me when I called before I left the office, but I hadn't added it to my list. I'd forgotten the artichoke hearts. My look of horror gave him his answer.

I stood up and began walking toward the kitchen. His words followed me.

"You didn't get them, did you?"

I turned the oven on, washed two large potatoes, rubbed them with olive oil, and placed them on the middle rack in the oven. Then I began unpacking the groceries. My husband stood just inside the kitchen door, glaring at me.

"Answer me!" he shouted.

"I'm sorry, dear," I replied meekly. "I forgot to write them on the list."

"So it's my fault, because I didn't tell you when you were writing your list at lunchtime! That's right! It's my fault!"

"I didn't say that. It's my fault. I forgot. I'm sorry." I was still speaking quietly.

He took a couple of steps toward me, and his voice was even louder this time. "Why can't you ever get anything right? Why do you provoke me? You're going to do this once too often. You're enough to make a saint swear!"

He took a couple more steps toward me, and I backed away.

"Don't walk away from me!" he said, coming right up to me. He put his hands on my shoulders and pushed me. I staggered backward, and my elbow hit the handle of the refrigerator. *Ouch!*

I took a step toward him and, surprising him, I put my hands on his shoulders and pushed him really hard, so that it was his turn to stagger backward.

He immediately raised his right hand and delivered a stinging blow across my face. I lunged sideways, then

45

headed across the kitchen, intent on grabbing the foot-long meat knife that stood with its smaller companions in a ceramic pot on the countertop. As I moved, I could feel the cool, solid handle in my hand; I could see the wide, sharp stainless steel blade gleaming.

I would stop him, once and for all! I was sick to death of this misery!

Just as I was reaching for the knife handle, I remembered where I was, and I came to my senses.

The year was 1980, and I was living in the United States of America! This was the country where the death penalty was still imposed for murder! Whoa! *Whoa!*

I turned and ran past my husband, into the garage, and out the garage door into the street.

He didn't follow me.

It was late spring, so the evening was pleasantly warm. I walked quickly down the darkening street. My mind was whirling. For the past ten years, every morning and every evening I had asked the Lord to make me wise, submissive, and loving, so that my husband would not get angry with me. Despite those prayers, I had spent many evenings out of the house, trying to escape his anger and desperately attempting to sort out what I had done to upset him and how to make amends. There was nothing unusual about what I was doing now. Unless we had guests, most evenings we would fight.

But there *was* something unusual about tonight. My miserable marriage had almost pushed me over the edge. The way I responded had both shocked and sobered me. *What on earth was I thinking? If I'd grabbed that deadly butcher knife, it would have taken only one downward blow to kill him! Lord, I'll bet you've given up on me now! How can you be working in this for good?*

I thought back to the recent past and remembered that this wasn't the first time during this marriage that homicide had entered my mind. Four years before, on

46

a holiday to Australia with my husband, we had visited my grandparents' abandoned nineteenth-century farmhouse.

I remembered a jar of white powder that they kept stored out of reach, high up on a door lintel in the bedroom I had slept in as a child. Its label said *arsenic*. When I was a little girl, my grandmother had pointed it out to me and explained that it was poison "for the rabbits." Alone for a moment, I wandered into my old bedroom and looked up. The jar, half-filled with white powder, was still there. I stood looking at it for a few minutes, wondering if I dared reach up and put it into my bag. Then I turned and walked away. Even though I put the thought out of my mind, it did come back from time to time after we returned to England.

Now, I was appalled and frightened by what I had almost done. As I walked, I decided that it was time for me to take an honest look at myself and at my situation.

This marriage, my second, had started badly. In 1968 I had volunteered to transfer from the Sydney, Australia, office to the Auckland, New Zealand, office of the legalistic religious group I belonged to and for which I was working. I intended to stay in New Zealand for just a year to heal and recover from several ill-fated romances. The atmosphere in the Auckland office was, to say the least, not pleasant. I was independent and outspoken and, as soon as I arrived, I immediately alienated the authoritarian man who was head pastor and office manager.

I determined, however, to enjoy my time in Auckland, despite his repressive attitude. I made friends easily, I had plenty of dates, there were lots of wonderful outdoor activities, and I was ready to explore every inch of the beautiful country in which I was privileged to be living. I had been there only a few months when a couple

47

of young men, who were recent university graduates, arrived to begin work as pastoral trainees.

One, who was younger than I, asked me out. I was twenty-six. He was barely twenty-one. I refused. "I'm too old for you. You should ask someone your own age," I told him.

However, he persisted. Finally, I said, "I'll go out with you this once."

He wasn't satisfied with "once." Once became twice, and he continued to politely plan dates, most of which I initially refused, only to give in after a couple of days.

At that time, one of the main tenets of the group was a belief in the imminent return of Christ—no later than 1975. Time was short. People lived in rented accommodations. They didn't bother to get their teeth fixed. Why waste money on things that had no eternal benefit?

Marriage outside the group was forbidden. Brief courtships were common. In this case, our courtship was discouraged, because of the acrimony between the head pastor and me. Beginning with my first conversation with this young man, the head pastor put obstacles in our way, punishing us both constantly. He expected the other staff members to spy on us and report back to him. This threw us together so that it became a "you and me against the world" relationship!

Just a little over a year after we first met, we married, reasoning, "Since the Lord is going to return soon, it's only for a few years. What harm can there be in that?" Within a couple of days, I realized that I had made an awful mistake. A "few years" might as well have been forever! I hadn't been aware that such misery existed in marriage. And I had no idea how much worse it would get.

This marriage was very different from my first marriage, which was a true love match. My first husband and I had met on my parents' farm. My dad had a friend,

Ken, who went hunting with him for rabbits, ducks, and foxes, or casting for brown trout as they sat on the creek bank. The summer I turned fourteen, Ken's young brother-in-law, Raymond, came with him. Over the next two summers, the three men hunted and fished together. After Christmas, while my mum was away visiting a sister, and I was at home with my siblings cooking for the family and helping with the wheat harvest, Raymond asked me out on a date.

I had met him briefly when he first came with Ken—but had rarely seen him since, and we had never talked. But I had "fallen in love" and was delighted when my dad said that I could take a day off and go to the city on a date with him. My father knew Raymond well and liked him. Though he was disappointed two years later when I wanted to marry instead of finish my teaching certificate, he gave us his blessing.

My first marriage was just like my parents' marriage. I was totally loved and cherished. I had autonomy and was treated with respect. I assumed that this was how all marriages were. Though I'd seen the misery in the homes of some of my school friends, I assumed that their parents' marriages were the exception. My relationship with Raymond was blissful, and every morning and every evening I uttered a prayer of thanksgiving and praise to the Lord for each day of happiness.

When Raymond died beside me in a horrific road accident less than six years later, I was totally devastated.

During my parents' marriage, they were gentle, loving, and indulgent. They never raised their voices to each other and rarely raised them to us, their children. Any raised voices we heard usually meant that there was a vociferous discussion going on or someone was being called in from outside. But I don't remember ever hearing either of them raise their voice in anger.

Raymond and I treated each other in the same way. He had spent the six years prior to our marriage living in barracks in the RAAF (Royal Australian Air Force). He was a gentle and easygoing peacemaker. Any time I was upset about something, he would just laugh softly and say quietly, "Sweetheart, let's sit down and talk calmly about this."

A couple of days after I married my second husband, while we were still on our honeymoon, I discovered how different this marriage was going to be. My new husband and I had chosen to honeymoon at a resort in the glorious Bay of Islands, on the northernmost tip of New Zealand's North Island.

We hadn't been there more than two days when I inadvertently did or said something that displeased him, and he exploded! He began shouting at me. I was frightened! I couldn't bear it, so I put my hands over my ears. That made him irate! He shouted louder. Then he grabbed my hands and pulled them away, and that frightened me even more. My legs buckled, and I fell to the floor in a heap, alternately sobbing and laughing hysterically. As I was falling, I grabbed at his hands, pulling him down with me. He hastily stood up, backed away, and looked at me scornfully.

"What are you doing?" he asked.

Finally, he walked out of the room.

When he returned about an hour later, I had washed my face and was sitting on the patio of the hotel, watching the sun slowly set over the Tasman Sea.

"What happened to you?" he asked.

"I guess I got frightened. I'm sorry," I replied. That was the end of the discussion.

One day, after the same kind of confrontation happened again, he told me that he was tired of me "faking" fear. I knew I wasn't faking. But his comment made me think.

50

My dad had taught his children fisticuffs. I was the eldest, and I learned very early to defend myself. "Up with your dukes," my dad would say, feigning a boxing stance and poking his clenched fist close to my face. By the time I was in school, I could bounce around an opponent, getting a fast right or left in under his defense. In my first few weeks of first grade, in the one-room schoolhouse I attended, one by one I vanquished three bullying sixth-grade boys with my "wicked right," bloodying their noses and thereby stopping them from stealing the lunches of kids my age.

As I recognized my fear of my husband, I began to think: *Those sixth-grade boys were frightening, but I overcame my fear enough to stand up to them. I don't have to be paralyzed by fear when someone shouts at me.* I decided that I'd stand up to my husband next time.

So, that's what I did. He shouted. Trembling with fear, I shouted back.

It didn't resolve the issue, but I no longer collapsed in a hysterical heap on the floor when he shouted at me. We went on with our lives as if nothing had happened. We never discussed it.

Some time later, in the middle of a shouting match, he walked over to me and pushed me. Startled, I staggered back. Then I left the house and went for a walk.

Next time, when he pushed me, I pushed him back.

Meanwhile, things were not going very well with the religious group. By early 1972 it was obvious that the predicted events leading up to the return of Jesus were not going to take place in time for his 1975 return. My husband and I began rethinking our lives. We bought land and built a house. It would be a few more years before the group admitted that they had it wrong, but we already knew. The head pastor was as obnoxious as ever to us both. At the end of 1973 we moved to England when the head pastor there offered my husband a job at their headquarters near London.

Back on his home turf, my husband's talents were being fully utilized for the first time, and he was relatively happy. Life was tranquil for a little while. But, after we were ousted from the group in 1976, things got tense again, and he started hitting me. It wasn't long before I defended myself—either by warding off the blows or by hitting him back.

I gradually became almost mute—both when I was alone with my husband and when we were in the company of others. We were both members of a large, charismatic Anglican church, but, nevertheless, I was afraid to talk to people in case I said the wrong thing. I couldn't confide in anyone. I lost my ability to laugh, to cry, and to think for myself. I explained, apologized, and covered up for my husband constantly. Truth, honesty, and integrity got lost in my efforts to make everything he did appear good. I didn't know what else to do. I was in a prison, and I didn't know how to get out!

In 1979 we moved to the United States.

Here I was, a few months later, forced to face the fact that my life was a mess. In my frustration and desperation, pushed to the limit, I had been only a split second away from trying to kill my husband with a butcher knife. What was I thinking? This was insanity. It could not go on.

Many times I had stayed up all night, sitting on the doorstep, walking up and down the street, or sitting in a darkened living room, trying to still my rapidly beating heart and the hammering that went on in my head, threatening to drive me out of my mind. Time after time I thought that I would go completely crazy. My life was so horrible it drove me to God—the only place I could find refuge, the only hope for my sanity. I knew that nothing could separate me from the love of God, and many times during those years all I had to cling to was the knowledge that he and I were one!

Every exchange between my husband and me ended up with my feeling that it was all my fault. If I could only find the correct combination of words, the right behavior, I would not provoke him, and all would be well. If only I were a "good wife," we would have a good marriage. I resolved to remember all the little things that peeved him and all the things that pleased him. After a few days, I would forget, and the whole thing would blow up again!

As I walked in the dark, leafy street near my home, pondering the impasse that my marriage had reached, his threat, "You're going to do this *once too often!* You're enough to make a saint swear!" echoed in my head.

In the early hours of the morning I crept into bed in a guest room on the first floor of our house. By the next morning I had decided that I had to lose myself in God and keep my distance from my husband. My only hope was, once again, to place the entire situation in the Lord's hands, trusting that he would give me the foresight and the wisdom to keep the peace.

I had to admit to myself that underlying everything was something I could do nothing about. I did not love my second husband in the wholehearted way that I had loved Raymond. I had never told him that—but I'm sure that he sensed it. He had the right to expect a wholehearted, sacrificial love. Without it, I had had no right to marry him in the first place.

I hoped that the Lord had a solution to our problem, because I didn't. It was beyond me!

Over the next few months, the distance between us widened. I brought friends home for meals or to stay overnight whenever I could. For the first time, I refused to accompany my husband on weekend business trips for the magazine, pleading too much work in the office. An uneasy peace gradually settled over our home.

Finally, he returned one Monday from a weekend business trip to make the announcement that he was in love with a woman he had just met and he wanted a divorce so that they could be married. He suggested I file immediately for a no-contest divorce—which I did—and then he left the following day to be with his fiancée and make plans for their future together.

I was not surprised that he wanted to exchange the misery we lived in for a love relationship, but I was devastated that I had failed so completely at marriage. To make my misery complete, the day he made his announcement was the anniversary of my first husband's death—a date that has always been particularly hard for me.

Within two months, the divorce was final. My marriage had ended. With its end, I began to grieve all the losses that I had experienced over the previous twenty years—losses for which I had never grieved. It was a long, slow process. I had no idea how much damage my Scarlett O'Hara attitude—"I'll think about it tomorrow"—had done to my psyche. But over the next few years, my precious, loving Lord slowly began to reveal to me how wounded I was and the way to healing and wholeness.

Perhaps, with early counseling, the marriage could have been saved. But we didn't discuss our problems with each other, much less with anyone else. No one knew what went on in our home. The marriage was not based on love—either romantic or sacrificial—and we had not expected it to last for a normal lifetime. We had expected it to last a few years at the most—not exactly the basis for a long and happy relationship! Oddly, throughout this ordeal, the thought of divorce had never crossed my mind. *Homicide* had but not divorce—not until I was forced into it.

In this marriage I learned about the pain, the desperation, and the loneliness that one can suffer. The emptiness I experienced when Raymond died was nowhere near as black and bleak as the sheer misery of bewilderment, fear, apprehension, and helplessness I felt every time my second husband's anger and frustration began exploding all around me.

I did not know what to do. When I was alone, I would sit numbly, wordlessly, in God's presence, hoping that he would change our circumstances in some way, perhaps perform a miracle and make everything right. He didn't perform any miracles. But, after I "got real" and admitted that the problem in my marriage was beyond me, our circumstances did begin to change, but not in the direction that I had in mind.

I turned around so that all I could do was face God. Then he made me look at myself. He made me acknowledge that I had made an awful mess of my life. He faced me with myself, and then he faced me with his unconditional love and approval of me—*just as I was.*

Do you have a horrible story like this? Do you feel that your life is such a mess that you are almost beyond God's blessings? The One who loves us tells us that *in all things* he works for our good (Rom. 8:28). Even before we turn to him, he is reaching out to us, offering us his forgiveness. He helps us forget our past, whatever it is. Whatever we have done, God has room in his heart for us. And he is just waiting for us to turn to him so that he can love us into wholeness. In Ezekiel—likening Jerusalem to an unloved, unwanted, abandoned newborn baby girl—God says:

> At birth, the very day you were born . . . No one *leaned kindly* over you. . . . You were exposed in the open fields;

you were *unloved*. . . . I saw you *struggling* . . . and I said to you . . . Live, and grow. . . . you grew, you reached marriageable age. . . . *Your time had come, the time for love.* . . . I made a covenant with you . . . and you became mine. I *bathed* you in water . . . I anointed you with oil . . . I loaded you with jewels . . . and dressed you in fine linen and embroidered silks. Your food was the finest flour, honey and oil. You grew more and more beautiful . . . because I had *clothed you with my own splendor.*

Ezekiel 16:4–14 JB

Another translation of "no one leaned kindly over you" is "no eye looked with pity on you" (NASB). Whichever one it is, it's God who "leans kindly" or "looks with pity." Our loving God picks us up—just as he picked up this abandoned one—cleans us up, and lavishes on us the gift of his love and his life.

God looks on us with compassion and steps in where no one else would. Whatever state we are in matters not to him; he loves us just the same. He rescues us from the mess we find ourselves in, bathes us in water, and sets us in the place that he has prepared for us—in his loving heart.

5

I Will Never Forsake You

I will never fail you nor forsake you . . .

Hebrews 13:5 NOAB

In desperation, late one damp, English autumn night in 1977, I had slipped out of the house in my nightgown and fled to the bank of the nearby river Ouse.

As I sat on the riverbank, I shivered. The dank night air was penetrating through my thin robe to my bare skin. I looked at the swiftly flowing, muddy river just ten feet away from the log I was sitting on, then I looked up at the merciless leaden sky. *Where are you, Lord? Don't you even care about me anymore?*

Then I stood up and, looking at the bleak sky again, I shouted, "You don't care! You won't even answer me! You'd let me jump into this wretched river, wouldn't you? It's been months since you've spoken!"

Dejected, I flopped down on the log again.

"Where are you, Lord? I threaten to play my 'trump card'—to end my life in this muddy river if you don't answer me—and still nothing happens," I sobbed. "I don't even know if you exist anymore. I don't know what to do!"

My heart felt as if it were breaking.
Where, oh, where, oh, where, are you, Lord?
I sat there in silence. The damp mist swirled about me, the muddy Ouse River slid silently by, and my clamoring spirit gradually became silent too.

Finally, I realized that as much as I wanted to escape the feelings of emptiness, I was not going to jump in the river that night. So I went up the riverbank and walked the several hundred yards along the dark road back to my home.

Over the next couple of weeks, I pondered the experience. For the previous few months I had pleaded with God to manifest himself again in my life the way he had done for years—through clear words and a definite feeling of his presence. But there was no response. During those months, my experience had made real for me the words in Leviticus 26:19 (NOAB): "heavens like iron" and "earth like brass." God didn't seem to be listening.

I had told God I would end it all if he didn't answer me. I thought he couldn't possibly ignore my threat. Well, I had discovered that he could ignore me—and he did! And I was sobered by it.

Now, I pondered, *what next?* He still wasn't answering me. God was still as distant as could be. I had no sense of his presence or even of his existence. After living most of my life with an almost constant awareness of his presence, these past few months without that awareness had been almost unbearable.

As I fussed and fumed and poured out my heart to the gray sky, the words of Job came to me, "Though he slay me, yet will I hope in him" (Job 13:15 NIV). *Yes, I agree with Job. Even if you never respond to me again, Lord, you can't get away from me. I love you and believe in you and I always will.*

After this experience on the bank of the river, I knew that I was not dealing with a distant God—but a very present one. I knew too that when God said, "I will never fail you nor forsake you" (Heb. 13:5 NOAB), he meant it. I was slowly beginning to realize that I was not dealing with a God who would allow me to continue to rely on my *feelings* about him. He wanted me to grow up, to be able to function without having to constantly check to see if he was there. He wanted me to *live by faith*.

For some time prior to this night, I had been an enthusiastic and active participant in a charismatic Anglican church. Sensing that there was more to living in the kingdom here and now than even my church's most exuberant celebrations, I blithely told the Lord, "This can't be all there is. There must be something more!" To my surprise and eventual dismay, the "more" became much less—the euphoric highs I had experienced in prayer and worship stopped, never to return!

After many months of silence and emptiness, in the midst of a particularly contentious patch in my marriage, I was desperate. That's why I had left the house in my nightgown and wandered down to the river's edge. After that night, I accepted God's silence, and I finally told him that I was ready for whatever he had for me. As I look back, I see so clearly that the unfailing love of God sustained, nourished, and comforted me in this dark journey and that he is with us in all the detours we take.

For the next couple of years, my relationship with God was mostly without any manifestations of his presence. Years later I was to see that this was my first taste of the incredible *mystery* of the love of God. He plunged me into a place in which all I had, most of the time, was my faith in him. Occasionally, however, I was encouraged and delighted when God graciously enveloped me in an unexpected moment of heartwarming love. The author of *The Cloud of Unknowing* speaks of this unexpected grace. He says: "[God] may touch you with a ray of his divine light which will pierce the *cloud of unknowing* between you and him."[1]

Early in 1979 I came across some magazines, published by a Christian organization, and I was amazed to find that there was a small group of evangelicals in the United States who accepted and taught what I had discovered a few years before—that my human spirit and the Spirit of Christ are one and that therefore the life I live is an incarnate life, Christ living in me.

On several occasions, in my small group at church, I had boldly stated that we were saints, not sinners, and that we lived in union with Christ. This thrilling truth, at least as I grasped it, was missed or rejected by most. After visiting the organization's summer camp in July and the annual conference in September, I had no doubt that my destiny was to be with this ministry.

Before the end of 1979, I was living in the Chicago area and responsible for the office of the magazine of which my husband was assistant editor. After we divorced in January 1981 and he left, I gradually took over his responsibilities in addition to my own. I began editing articles for the magazine, occasionally wrote one, and attended all the conferences and camps sponsored by the magazine's parent organization.

I felt that the magazine needed to publish articles from a broader variety of authors and that new books needed to be added to its book list. This was done, and editorially it became more ecumenical.

As the book list expanded, I puzzled over some of the books, reading and rereading them, sensing that there was something that I was missing. One in particular that I went back to time and time again was Madame Guyon's *Experiencing the Depths of Jesus Christ*. What was I missing? I was aware that God's answer to my heart's desire for intimacy with him might come from outside my current experience. I was *looking* for something. I just wasn't sure what it was.

I sensed that hidden away in the talk about "Christ in you" (Col. 1:27) and our being "one spirit with him" (1 Cor. 6:17) was the way to love. I wanted a personal, intimate relationship with Jesus. I wanted more than *knowing about* being "one with him"—I wanted the *experience* of it.

Around and around in my head went the question: *Being one—in union—means what? Is it just an intellectual assent to a truth or is it a fact? Is it a concept or is it an experience?* Being a Christian means that the Spirit of Christ lives in me (1 Cor. 3:16 NIV). Okay, that's a fact. So what? What difference does it make? It makes a difference as far as my eternal—future—life is concerned, but what about my here-and-now life? I can say, "I'm one with Christ," but does an awareness of this truth *change* me? Once again, it was Paul's talk of love—of its being the most excellent of spiritual gifts (see 1 Cor. 12–13)—that challenged me.

What difference would the *experience of union*—as opposed to *knowledge about union*—make? In marriage the experience of union makes all the difference. Knowing about union would never result in a child, but the *experience* of union very well could. Much of the talk about union sounded to me like little children playing house. I wanted to go beyond "playing house" with God. I longed to live in union with Christ.

A few months after my husband and I divorced, as I drove west to work early one morning, with the rising sun at my back and a pale gold and pink sky in front of me, I was sobbing and banging my hand on the steering wheel and crying out to the Lord as I drove. "I am *so* unhappy, Lord. Instead of making my life better, you've just let it get worse and worse. Here I am, trying to survive alone, working two jobs just to make the mortgage payments. The kitchen tap is dripping and needs replacing. My car has broken down [I had borrowed a 1965 Ford pickup that was so old it not only had a stick-shift, but the driver had to double-clutch to change gears!], and *you don't even care!*"

I was approaching a traffic light, so I slowed the truck down and changed into a lower gear in the hope that the light would turn green before I reached it.

"You are not being very nice to me! You call this love?" I shouted. "I divorce you!"

I looked up at the sky. And then I heard it, and I couldn't believe my ears! Laughter. *Laughter,* of all things! Not sympathy!

Divorce me, will you? To whom will you go then?

And there was that tender chuckle again!

I realized that I had nowhere to go. I was stuck with God. Through my tears, I began to laugh. "Oh, Lord. You win! We're stuck with each other!"

From that time on I knew that despite the fog I was in, there was no way to get away from God; we were "stuck with each other." It was to be a number of years before the fog cleared completely, but it did clear. Until that time all I knew was that God had hold of me, and that he would never, ever fail me or forsake me.

I began to look for a church home, and this search went on for seven years. Finally, I walked into a church one day, and within a few minutes I knew that, at last, I had found the place for me. It was there, in that environment, that the answer to my desire for "something more"—for intimacy with the Lord—was to come. It came from an unexpected source, from my exposure to a program that nurtured the religious experience of children. It led me into what my heart longed for—into the experience of a living union with God through the practice of silent, wordless prayer.

Part 2

How to Be . . .
Quiet in His Presence

Why should I spend an hour in prayer when I do nothing during that time but think about people I am angry with, people who are angry with me, books I should read and books I should write, and thousands of other silly things that happen to grab my mind for a moment?

The answer is: because God is greater than my mind and my heart, and what is really happening in the house of prayer is not measurable in terms of human success and failure.

What I must do first of all is be faithful. If I believe that the first commandment is to love God with my whole heart, mind, and soul, then I should at least be able to spend one hour a day with nobody else but God. The question as to whether it is helpful, useful, practical, or fruitful is completely irrelevant, since the only reason to love is love itself. Everything else is secondary.

The remarkable thing, however, is that sitting in the presence of God for one hour each morning—day after day, week after week, month after month—in total confusion and with myriad distractions radically changes my life. God, who loves me so much that he sent his only Son not to condemn me but to save me, does not leave me waiting in the dark too long. I might think that each hour is useless, but after thirty or sixty or ninety such useless hours, I gradually realize that I was not as alone as I thought; a very small, gentle voice has been speaking to me far beyond my noisy place.

So: Be confident and trust in the Lord.

Henri J. M. Nouwen
The Road to Daybreak

6

Steps to Being Quiet
in His Presence

Be still, and know that I am God.

Psalm 46:10 NIV

How does one become quiet in God's presence? How do you do silent prayer? Well, it's a lot like learning to swim. You can be told how water feels and what to do once you get into it, but unless you take the plunge, you won't know what it is to swim. It will remain a mystery to you.

Teaching centering prayer—contemplative prayer—in today's cultural context can be likened to teaching swimming to desert dwellers who've never seen a decent waterhole, much less a swimming pool. After a brief explanation of what water feels like, and what it can do, the next best thing is to get into the water and begin to learn to swim.

The same is true of the prayer of silence. Words alone about how to do this prayer are not enough. The only way to know God in this intimate way is to do it—to experience his love through silent prayer. Just trust God, take the plunge into his loving presence, and begin to learn from him, the meek and lowly One (Matt. 11:29 KJV).

In 1988 I decided to begin a training course in the Catechesis of the Good Shepherd, a Montessori-based religious experience for children aged three to twelve years. The summer camp I attended included quite a few small children, and the woman who usually worked with them had quit. Two colleagues and I volunteered to fill the gap, and we wondered if there was a better way of teaching the little children about a loving God than through the retelling of scary Old Testament stories and memorizing Scriptures. I thought the Good Shepherd program might be the answer. My church had used the Catechesis for many years and so, before I began the course, I thought it wise to spend a Sunday morning as an observer in the Catechesis atrium.

My favorite space was the "prayer corner" in the room for the three- to five-year-olds. On a little table was a cross flanked by two candles, a vase of flowers, and a white statue of the Good Shepherd with a lamb over his shoulder. Several small reproductions of classic religious art hung on the wall at a small child's eye level. On the floor there were pastel-colored cushions and a little basket filled with small flash cards on which were written words of praise and love, such as "I love you," "Praise God," "Be still," "Bless you," "Jesus," "Lord," and "Father." Adults read these words quietly to the children if asked to do so, and then each child was left alone in the prayer corner.

In the Catechesis program, the space is specially set up to foster worship and to teach the essentials of Christianity through tangible but indirect means. Adults are trained to primarily *observe* the children, allowing them to nurture their relationship with God without unnecessary words and without the adult intruding into the child's contemplation. The emphasis of the program is, "Help me to come to God by myself."[1]

Over the next few months, I worked with the children in the atrium on Sundays, while I did the training course for that age group. I loved the focus on the unconditional love of the Good Shepherd for his sheep and the way it nurtured the child's natural response of love and thankfulness to the Good Shepherd. I found myself beginning to respond in the same way.

Even though the Scriptures are read to the children, the child's relationship with God as well as the child's sense of awe and wonder at God's great love and goodness are what are encouraged. The children sit in the quiet spaces in the room for as long as they need to, pondering the wonders of the Lord. Gradually, as I watched these little children worship, I became comfortable with silence, and I became aware of how powerfully the Lord speaks to us through it.

The next year my church had a contemplative prayer workshop, which I eagerly attended. I was quite amazed at the depth of personal communion with God I felt in that silent communal atmosphere. There was something powerful and very touching about twenty or so seekers of God spending an evening and the next day together without speaking to each other till the end. We had all agreed to turn our eyes and our hearts toward God for that period of time, and I found, to paraphrase John Wesley, that my heart was strangely warmed by the experience. It did not occur to me, however, that the prayer of silence could be an everyday practice. At that point I saw it only as a special retreat experience.

Then in 1990 I discovered—in M. Basil Pennington's wonderful book *Centering Prayer*[2]— four simple steps to aid in the daily practice of the prayer of silence. Instead of having to fight the "I don't know how to pray" syndrome and the "I don't have the words for this one" excuse, I was presented with a way to pray in which words and concepts were ignored.

I found this strange and different but I sensed freedom! Maybe this was the "something more" about which I had long before questioned the Lord. Like a duck to water, I *plunged* into this prayer of unknowing. I began immediately—sitting for twenty minutes in silent, contemplative prayer. And I loved it! At first, I started my time of contemplative sitting by silently saying to myself a Scripture used in the prayer corner with the little children: "*Be still,* and know that I am God" (Ps. 46:10 NIV). After a little while, I found my own "love word."

In the prayer of silence, one is encouraged not to pay attention to any words or thoughts that come to mind but to simply set them aside for the time. The purpose, or intent, of the prayer is to be with our Lord—to be *with* the One we are meant to adore and worship. We come to him for *himself.* We enter into the Trinity's "circle of love," empty-handed, humble, and speechless, anticipating the total acceptance for which our hearts yearn.

As I began to practice contemplative prayer, I discovered that it is a prayer anyone can do. Whether it is for twenty minutes, ten minutes, or five minutes once or twice a day, it's a prayer for everyone. I didn't have to wait until I'd read everything I could find out about it or until I'd checked it out with my mentors. It was so simple, so accessible. It seemed that the best way to learn it was just to get started and do it! Just like learning to swim, after a brief explanation of the basic steps, it's time to take the plunge!

Here, in my words, are the four steps I used and found so helpful.

1. Become quiet, both within and without. We quiet our bodies and sit comfortably with our eyes closed.
2. Turn within. We turn our attention to the Lord, giving ourselves to him as a gift. For the next few minutes we are all his. In faith we trust that he is here, present with us, accepting us, loving us.
3. Use a chosen "love word." Whenever we catch ourselves paying attention to one of the myriad thoughts that race through our heads, we simply and gently murmur our word as a symbol of our intention to be still in the Lord's presence.
4. End gently by slowly repeating a favorite, familiar prayer. A prayer, such as the Lord's Prayer, is a gentle transition back into our busy, noisy world.

Whenever prayer is mentioned, we automatically think of words—spoken or unspoken—of praise, petition, intercession, or repentance. But centering prayer does not involve words. In this wordless prayer of unknowing, we are not simply sitting in silence while our minds continue to pray. We turn within, and actually *lay aside* all words and thoughts. We do not attempt to empty our minds of thoughts. That's impossible. But we go beyond thoughts, words, and emotions. We open our hearts, our whole beings, to God.

This is a time to give ourselves to God in love. We come to him without an agenda—no words of praise or petition or penitence; those are for another time when we pray different kinds of prayer. In contemplative prayer we come simply to *be* with God, to worship and adore him in silence, totally surrendered to him in love, resting in him.

There are two important things we should do before beginning our time of sitting in silence with the Lord. First, we decide how long to sit—and stick to it. It's bet-

69

ter not to make it too long to begin with—start with five or ten minutes, rather than twenty minutes—only to get discouraged and give up. Second, we need to choose a love word or, as Basil Pennington calls it, a prayer word. This is a word or phrase that we use to help us return to our intention to be silent before the Lord without distraction. Words, such as *God, Lord, Father, Abba, love, peace, rest, cherish, bask, gaze, home*—or phrases, such as *Have mercy, I love you, Be still*—are commonly used. Choose a word or phrase that is meaningful to you and don't worry about getting it right. You can trust the Lord to show you which one is best for you.

Whenever I share centering prayer with people in a retreat or workshop, the comment I hear the most is about how hard it is for us to still our active minds. When you find distracting thoughts crowding in, recall your love word and say it slowly, reminding yourself of your intention to be with God. Your love word or phrase is a symbol of that intention. It is not a mantra. It has no power in itself. It is simply a way to bring you back to inner silence.

When you realize you've been distracted, be very compassionate with yourself. Say your love word slowly and gently, just like a murmur or a sigh of love. Your intention to give yourself to God as a gift, to rest in him, to be silent with him is what you affirm when you use your love word. He already knows your heart's intention, and he is infinitely patient with you. Like the mother of a newborn, he does not expect a faultless performance.

Laying aside our thoughts is no easy process. Initially you will be amazed at how much inner "noise" there is. There is an incessant monologue going on. But that's normal. It's true for everyone. If you think you are an extreme case, consider this. It is said that the average person has sixty thousand thoughts a day!

Whatever you do, don't worry about the inner noise. Don't assume that you "are not good" at contemplative prayer when you become aware, for the first time, of all those thoughts. You will find that they're always there. The mind was made to think, just as the body was made to breathe. You can't stop the thoughts, so don't try. Don't *do* anything. Just don't pay any attention to them.

I was amazed at myself when I first began this prayer. I thought that I was an introvert who loved silence, but I didn't realize how much was going on in my head until I decided not to pay attention to my thoughts! As soon as I sat down, closed my eyes, and became still, the unruly thoughts began demanding my attention! I couldn't believe it! I thought I must be doing it wrong! I felt guilty. Then, I thought, *This isn't for me.* But I kept feeling drawn back to try again. More than once, I tried to do extra time to make up for the minutes that I thought had been a complete waste!

Then I realized that God was smiling at me! He was not interested in my *performance.* He was interested in *me.* He saw my intention. He had no report card. He wasn't grading me! He loves me and wants to be with me for *myself,* and he wants me to come and be with him for *himself,* just like any lover! Persisting with my time of sitting, going into the silence beyond thought, regardless of the inner noise, has taught me to *be still*— to be still and pay no attention to my clamoring thoughts.

Even now, distracting and guilty thoughts still come rushing in. But I am ready for them! I simply murmur my love word and return to my original intention to be still in the presence of God. When the time is up, I say the Lord's Prayer, and then, sometimes, if it's been a particularly "noisy" day, I say, "Thank you, Lord, that you love me and that you don't keep score!"

71

The author of *The Cloud of Unknowing* says of contemplative prayer, "Your undisciplined faculties, finding no meat to feed upon, will angrily taunt you to abandon it. They will demand that you take up something more worthwhile."[3] Don't give up, even if you find at first that sitting in silence is a little difficult. Most people do. In fact it's often quite uncomfortable. Our natural mind won't give up without a fight—so don't be surprised. We rush out of our busy world into our contemplative prayer time, and we find that it takes a little while to settle down into the silence. Sometimes we may spend the entire time struggling to be quiet within. It's best to stay for the intended time, if possible, resisting the temptation to see this struggle as a waste of time or condemn ourselves as failures at this prayer. The intention to give ourselves to God is what he sees. Being faithful to that intention despite apparent failure creates within us a place of silence that we can return to at any time.

Some of us find that not only our thoughts—our "undisciplined faculties"—taunt us, urging us to give up this foolishness of listening for what cannot be heard, but even some of our most trusted and beloved mentors will frown on the prayer of silence. These dear Christian friends think that we are going too far—being silent when there is so much work to do, so many good causes to pray for! If you are being called to this prayer as Mary of Bethany was, remember the words of Jesus when Martha questioned him: "Mary has chosen the good part, which shall not be taken away from her" (Luke 10:42).

Committing ourselves to the addition of silent prayer to our personal devotional life is good, but we need to be aware that silent prayer is a faith practice with few measurable results. Lest you become discouraged in the early stages and give up, it's best to find a group—or at least one experienced contemplative—with whom to "sit in silence" on a regular basis.[4]

Like desert dwellers getting into water and learning to swim, we beginners in contemplative prayer are in unfamiliar territory. But don't be discouraged. As the slogan says, "Just do it!" Take the time daily to be still, whether it's for twenty minutes, ten minutes, or five minutes. As you immerse yourself regularly in the silence of unknowing, you will find that you are not sitting there alone. The One who loves you has been waiting for you all along, and he is delighted that you have set aside the cares of this life for a few minutes to rest in him.

7

Resting in God

Jesus said, "Come to me, all who labor and are heavy laden. . . . Take my yoke upon you . . . and *you will find rest for your souls.*"

Matthew 11:28–29 NOAB

Springtime on the farm was lambing season—so it was an exciting but anxious time for my family. It was exciting as we waited for the first lambs to be born; it was anxious because during the day, crows and eagles hovered overhead, and at night, foxes prowled, waiting to catch an unwary sheep alone with her new lamb.

My dad walked around the paddocks, closely watching his flock of Merinos, as the ewes grew larger and larger. Finally, the day came when he gently removed the largest sheep, one by one, and put them in the house paddock. Years of experience told him that these larger ewes would probably have twins and would need special protection and perhaps extra care.

The ewes could rest safely in the small paddock near the house, because our sheepdogs were tethered day and night on the perimeter to deter predators. Neither foxes nor crows have any scruples about killing a newborn lamb while the mother is occupied with the birth of a twin, but the presence of the dogs would keep them at bay. The little vulnerable flock always clustered under the enormous eucalyptus trees near the house, and from the kitchen windows my mum could keep watch over them for most of the day.

At night Dad hung lighted lanterns on the fences, and usually he would be up several times to quietly patrol the outer edge of the paddock. After a few weeks, safely delivered of their twins, the ewes—now strong enough to protect themselves from predators—would return with their lambs to the flock.

It was not unusual during that time for my father, often dripping and bedraggled from being out in a sudden spring shower, to walk into the warm kitchen carrying in his arms a motionless newborn lamb wrapped in a saddle blanket or a wheat sack or just under his coat. The cats on the hearth in front of the glowing woodstove would be unceremoniously displaced by a small box, into which the pitiful little bundle would be gently placed and covered with a dry, old towel. Often a little brandy mixed with warm water would be administered.

Then would begin a round-the-clock watch as each member of the family took turns trying to warm the cold, damp lamb by gently rubbing it with a rough, dry towel to stimulate its circulation, and regularly putting a milk-moistened finger to its mouth to see if it would try to suckle. Almost always, within an hour, we would be elated to hear a feeble bleat coming from the box. Shortly after that, the shaky little creature would learn to drink warmed milk from a bottle. After a day or two, the lamb would be strong enough to be reunited with its mother or put in the shed with the orphans.

My dad knew what was best for his sheep, and he also knew how vulnerable they were. I think this is why, when I began working with little children in the Catechesis of the Good Shepherd at my church, I found pondering scriptural references to the Good Shepherd and his flock particularly meaningful. I began to think about sheep and what I had witnessed as a child. Now, after many years, I was looking back, and I realized how much I had absorbed from my childhood and how rich was that time.

In the quiet environment of the Catechesis program, all were encouraged to wonder about the Good Shepherd and his relationship to us. One of my favorite verses has always been one in Isaiah. After speaking about God coming "in power," it says: "He is like a shepherd feeding his flock, gathering lambs in his arms, holding them against his breast and leading to their rest the mother ewes" (Isa. 40:11 JB).

It was easy for me to relate to this, as I had seen Dad and Mum gently taking care of the flock. The Good Shepherd has power, but he's also very tender and gentle. He feeds his flock, gathers the helpless lambs in his arms, and holds them close where they are warm and safe. He leads the ewes out of danger into safety and rest. He takes care of everything.

Jesus said, "Come to me. . . . Take my yoke upon you . . . and you will find rest for your souls" (Matt. 11:28–29). For years I had known that God's love for me was infinite, tender, and unconditional. But *knowing* his love and *experiencing* rest in it are two different things. Only when I obeyed his voice and began to come to him in the silence of the prayer of love did my soul begin to find rest. Until then I rarely experienced rest; I was too busy, bursting with ideas, plans, activities, and energy. I found that it is in the silence that my tender, gentle God holds me close to his heart. It's when I'm exhausted, afraid, heartbroken, or about to give up that he comforts me and restores my soul.

I have found that my regular times of stillness and silence have made me more aware in every area of my life of the gentle whisper of my ever-present Lover. Deep in my spirit, he nudges me to be a lover too. As my awareness of my loving Lord has deepened, so too has my awareness of his intimate involvement in all the details of my daily life. These words of Scripture have gradually become real to me: "He who is your teacher will hide no longer. . . . Whether you turn to right or left, your ears will hear these words behind you, 'This is the way, follow it'" (Isa. 30:20–21 JB). I don't "hear" words! What happens could be best described simply as an *impression*.

In the past, I would probably have been too busy, too frantic, too "noisy" to notice—as I rushed around trying to stay in charge of every area of my life. Now, throughout each day, I allow myself to stop and enjoy little oases of quiet. I find myself constantly being reminded of things to do, people to call, books to read. Each day, over and over again, I realize that a particular thought did not come from me. It came from the One who loves me dearly and with whom I am in intimate communion. Then I am quick to say, "Thank you, my Love, for waking me up to that! Thank you!"

In my daily talking prayer—not my silent prayer—I become aware of the gentle whispers of the Beloved speaking in my heart. The self-centered monologue-type of prayer (me talking nonstop) begins to give way to a prayer that is more like a dialogue. I speak and then rest. At times, a particular prayer request or person may come to my attention and I find myself totally at a loss for words to pray. That's when I mentally hold the person up before the Lord and pray Brennan Manning's *prayer of belonging:* "Abba, I belong to you. Abba, _____ belongs to you."[1] In praying this, I recognize that only God knows the heart and faith of another. I don't know how to pray for them. Before I go on with my verbal prayer, or rush off to my other activities, I rest for a while in the wonder of Abba's love for us, holding in my heart and mind this person who belongs to God.

A dear woman of my acquaintance is one of those people whom you dare not greet with, "How are you?" Her reply is always a resigned sigh, and then one word, "Tired!"

Just speaking to her seems to make the tiredness rub off on me. She's a hardworking Christian woman who is full of good deeds, but, like Martha of Bethany, she is "worried and bothered about so many things" (Luke 10:41), and she needs the rest for her soul that Jesus offers us.

As we come to Jesus, take his yoke upon us, and find rest—in other words, we begin to live the contemplative life, rather than just having an occasional contemplative experience—we must look at our entire devotional life. Silent contemplative prayer grows out of a deepening relationship with God, so the time after all the words are said is a good time to be silent before the Lord. I find, however, that my time of silence is best as my first activity of the day (and the last before I go to sleep). The other parts I usually do before breakfast, though they can be cut short and done at another time. Each of us needs to find the sequence of these devotions that works best for us. In addition to our daily prayers and Scripture readings, we should consider reflecting on our lives in the light of Scripture and praying verbally in response to that reading and reflection.[2] Reflecting on God's greatness and goodness and our littleness and sinfulness will usually help us get things in perspective. We recognize where we have fallen short, ask forgiveness, and rejoice in the grace and mercy God extends to us.

78

Looking ahead to the One who was to bring that grace and mercy to us, the Lord speaks through Isaiah: "Here is rest. . . . Here is repose." But, we are told, "They would not listen" (Isa. 28:12). Paul, in Acts, speaks of the need to *repent* and *return* to the Lord for rest, for refreshment: "Repent therefore and return, so that your sins may be wiped away, in order that times of refreshing may come from the presence of the Lord" (Acts 3:19).

The promise here, if we will listen, repent, and return to the Lord's presence, is that we will be refreshed! I've found this to be true. Practicing the presence of God, through the prayer of silence, is *refreshing*. It is only as I let go of my agenda, cast all my burdens on him, and come to him that I find rest for my soul. My clamoring spirit gradually becomes quiet, and all my anxious words melt away as I give myself up to his loving presence.

Even if I come to my contemplative prayer time filled with worries and anxieties and instead of being still, spend the entire time gnawing my lip and fussing, he's not keeping score on me. He's not keeping track of how well I do this prayer or of the good and bad things that I do or have done. Maybe I am—but he's not. He doesn't care. His relationship with me, his love for me, is not dependent on anything I do or don't do. He's concerned for my well-being. He offers me rest. He offers restoration.

One of my Australian friends tells of returning south to Victoria after wintering in the warmer north for three months. The Australian gum tree is not deciduous; it doesn't drop its leaves, but it does shed bark and dead branches. Pauline's garden, therefore, was knee-deep in litter from her numerous gum trees. Early on the first morning, as she sat down for her twenty minutes of contemplative prayer, she kept being distracted by the thought of the mess outside that would take hours to clear away. Finally, she said, "Lord, sitting here with you is not getting my garden cleaned up!"

Pauline seemed to hear him respond, "You stay here with me! I'll take care of it!"

So she stayed. After a few more minutes of wrestling with her thoughts, she found herself resting in his presence.

A little later she was finishing up the dishes in the sink when a cheery voice called, "Anyone home?" and into her kitchen walked two old friends from the nearby town. "The Lord told us to come around with our ute [utility truck, i.e., pickup] and help you clean up your garden, so here we are!" the wife said, grinning broadly as she and her husband stood there, waiting for Pauline's greeting.

Out into the garden the three of them went, and by lunchtime most of the bark and branches had been cleared and loaded onto their vehicle to be hauled away.

Pauline's concluding comment was, "So I guess the Lord showed me that sitting with him comes first!"

Maybe this is where the repenting and returning fit in. We are so sure that our agenda is right. We are so inflexible. We are convinced that the activities we are involved in won't survive without us.

But just try it. Try putting a little silent prayer first on your agenda. Take the Lord up on his offer to come to him and find rest. He longs for us to come and bask in his presence. He frequently surprises us with benefits of being in his presence *in this life*—even though that shouldn't be our primary motivation for giving ourselves to him in silence.

I'm still bursting with ideas, plans, and activities. But I now know how to stop. I know how to do absolutely nothing. Now, I regularly practice just being still in God's presence, coming to him with no agenda, no words, no good thoughts—I come to just *be,* and I'm not disappointed. I do find rest for my soul.

It's easier, now, to be *still* on the road when I'm stopped by a red light. Instead of banging my hand on the steering wheel, willing the light to change so I can rush off again, I rest until the light turns green. Most of the time now I can stand quietly and patiently in the checkout line, often praying, "Lord, have mercy," as I look at the harried faces of other shoppers. I notice the flowers on the trees in spring, the sparrows gathering wisps of dead grass for their nest, and the people who regularly walk their little dogs on my street. I'm surprised by how much I see now—so many things I was in too much of a hurry to see before I began to practice resting in the Lord.

As I give up my need to always be in a hurry and to always be in control, I begin to see more clearly my smallness and God's greatness. As I see God's greatness, I am thankful that Jesus said, "Come to Me. . . . and . . . find rest for your souls." I need to find rest in this life. My family and friends can certainly attest to that!

I wince as I read the words of Paul in Romans: "Strive together with me in your prayers . . . that I may come to you . . . and find *refreshing* rest in your company" (Rom. 15:30, 32). "Find refreshing rest" in *my* company? How about you? Are you *refreshing* to be with? With a little embarrassment, I think of all the years that just the opposite of this would have been said of me! How exhausting to be around someone who knows nothing of inner rest or peace!

God promises us a new and tender heart, one that is no longer restless. As I come home to the Lord, my restlessness is gradually replaced with a quiet peace.

The gift of rest and peace is offered to all. We are invited to come to him, with open hands and an open heart, and give ourselves to him in the prayer of surrender, the prayer of silence. Let's respond to Jesus, the Good Shepherd, who is calling us to come to him and find rest for our souls.

8

Becoming like a Little Child

He called a little child and had him stand among them.
And he said: "I tell you the truth, unless you change and
become like little children, you will never enter the kingdom of heaven."

Matthew 18:2–3 NIV

Have you ever watched a small child build a sand cas-
tle or do a puzzle or write a story? This child has no
doubts about his being made in the image of the Creator. Every step the child takes and every move he makes
shows that he is secure in his identity as a creative person. The child can paint and draw, compose songs, play
the piano, and solve all the mysteries of the universe—
beginning with the small burdened ant that just crossed
his path!

Unhampered by the fear of not living up to someone's
expectations and unconcerned about how he looks to
his peers, the small child plunges headlong into every
exciting challenge that comes along. His creative activities don't have to have any worthwhile result, nor do

they even have to be useful. The family reacts with delight and surprise at everything the child does, urging him on to greater adventures. The child feels unconditionally loved and knows the joy of being with those who are thrilled with him in every way.

We adults are made in the image of God, just as surely as is the small child. But we still have a lot to learn from small children.

At the annual summer camp I attended in Wisconsin, two colleagues and I had turned a small three-room cabin into a "children's house." While the adults were busy with camp meetings, about forty children were left in our care. We devised a religious program that was loosely based on Montessori principles. We set up each of the three adjoining rooms of the cabin for a specific age group: three- to five-, six- to eight-, and nine- to eleven-year-olds. Materials used were minimal, as everything had to be transported with us from our homes in Chicago. The children quickly felt at home in the children's house, absorbing the few rules and settling comfortably into the space, often spending most of the day there, even when the program itself was over.

In the room for three-to-five-year-olds, the bare cement floor was covered with pastel-colored carpet samples. In one corner sat a small, white-lace-covered table. On it was a candle in a tiny candlestick, a small vase with real flowers, a small gold cross on a stand, and an open Bible. Around the table were scattered large, soft, colored cushions.

Set out on a low shelf for the children's use were containers filled with crayons, freshly sharpened colored pencils, and crisp white sheets of paper. Beside a group of glue pots was a flat tray with little stacks of cut-up colored paper sorted by color for collage.

Early one morning I sat quietly watching as the children came into the children's house before our program for the day began. A little three-year-old boy was choosing the "work" he wanted to do. He picked up a small table and set it down, got a tray, placed a sheet of paper on it, and then carefully selected his colored pencils, one for each color of the rainbow. He sat at his table and, holding all the pencils vertically with the lead pointing down onto the paper, he slowly and deliberately began to draw. In the middle of the sheet of paper, he drew a small circle and, never lifting the pencils from the paper, kept drawing in ever-widening circles. He was totally absorbed in his task.

He was about halfway through when an older child from one of the other rooms walked over to him and said quietly, "Jamie, you know the rule! You're only supposed to take three pencils at a time! You need to put all but three back."

Jamie's hand stopped moving. He glanced up momentarily, looked around distractedly, and then he went back to his slow, deliberate drawing. Only when he reached the outer edge of the paper with his multicolored circles did he look up again. He sighed, stood up, walked to the pencil box with his pencils, and put all but one back. Then he picked up his piece of paper and came over to me.

"Would you write my name on this, please?" he asked, handing me the piece of paper and the pencil. Then he looked me straight in the eye and said quietly, "These are all the colors that make up God!"

As I looked at him, I realized that I hadn't had a clue about what he had been doing. But now I saw, and I found myself covered with goose bumps! Wow! When had *I* last seen God as an awesome multicolored Light! Little Jamie, with his child heart, was completely confident in the importance of the "work"—the worship—

in which he had been so absorbed; it was so important that he had no time to pay attention to "rules" that got in the way of his completing it!

In Mary of Bethany, sitting at Jesus' feet when he came to visit, we see the same single-minded attention and confidence and the same lack of interest in rules or in what others thought. In *The Cloud of Unknowing* the author points out that Mary's focus was on the Lord, not on herself. She forgot whether "she had been sinner or innocent" and "became oblivious of everything, both material and spiritual." This is how he describes her:

> Mary turned to Jesus with all the love of her heart, unmoved by what she saw or heard spoken and done about her. She sat there in perfect stillness with her heart's secret, joyous love intent upon that *cloud of unknowing* between her and her God. . . . And it was to this very cloud that Mary directed the hidden yearning of her loving heart. . . . Even when Martha complained to Jesus about her . . . Mary remained there quite still and untroubled . . . for she was utterly absorbed in another work, all unknown to Martha, and she did not have time to notice her sister or defend herself.[1]

As I read this, I see Jamie. He "sat there in perfect stillness" except for the slow, deliberate movement necessary to get the colors onto the paper. He had no time to worry about the rules. He was absorbed in expressing what his heart had told him was true about God. He was obeying a higher law. Like Mary, who remained there "quite still and untroubled," even when Martha complained to Jesus about her, Jamie ignored the voice of criticism. He remained unperturbed, because he was "utterly absorbed in another work, all unknown" to those around him. He did not answer his critic or try to defend himself. He knew what had to be done. Once

This story in John 12 is a different Mary.

done, then he would pay attention to the rules. Like Mary, this small child allowed himself to be totally absorbed in what was most important to him.

In both the story of Mary sitting at the Lord's feet while sister Martha does all the work and the one in which she uses an entire container of expensive ointment to anoint the Lord (John 12:3 NIV), we see this total concentration on her object of adoration. When the disciples are indignant at the extravagant waste of the perfume—protesting that it could have been sold and the money given to the poor—Jesus tells them, "Leave her alone. She has done a beautiful thing to me. . . . she did it to prepare me for burial" (Matt. 26:10, 12 NIV). The disciples' logic told them that caring for the poor was the right thing to do; but Mary caught a glimpse of who Jesus was, and her response was one of love, not logic.

A little time before this, the disciples had tried to stop parents from bringing their small children to Jesus, only to have Jesus say: "Let the little children come to Me; do not stop them; for it is to such as these that the kingdom of heaven belongs. . . . anyone who does not welcome the kingdom of God like a little child will never enter it" (Luke 18:16 JB). The disciples missed the point, just as they had missed it earlier when, after arguing among themselves about who was the greatest, they put the question to Jesus: "Who is the greatest in the kingdom of heaven?" (Matt. 18:1 NIV).

Scripture tells us how Jesus responded: "He called a little child and had him stand among them. And he said, 'I tell you the truth, unless you change and *become like little children*, you will never enter the kingdom of heaven.'" He said to them, "Whoever *humbles himself* like this child is the greatest in the kingdom of heaven" (Matt. 18:2–4 NIV).

What was Jesus doing? How do adults *become like little children?* How does one *humble oneself?* Jesus was giving a show-and-tell lesson to the disciples by setting a little child in their midst as a visible example.

Didn't God give us a dramatic visible example of humility in the lowly beginnings of the Carpenter of Nazareth? Dare we meditate on that for a moment? Dare we set aside all the trappings of our sophisticated world and imagine ourselves in the company of a few poor shepherds and a handful of farm animals in a dimly lit cave? Dare we immerse ourselves in the miracle and the paradox of the incarnation and ponder its meaning? Dare we *become as little children* again and enter that world of awe and adoration? Dare we forget ourselves completely, focus on God, and worship him for himself?

Where in us is the wonder that fills a child who observes a flower that has just opened, a golden honeybee as she gathers pollen, a flaming-red cardinal singing in the highest tree, a blue-and-black butterfly flitting from brilliantly colored flower to flower? Where are we when all these miracles are going on around us? Do we ever stoop to smell the roses like a little child? Do we stop in our tracks and greet with glee another human being, a walking miracle? Usually, no! It's sad that, all too often, we are too busy to take time to acknowledge the handiwork of the Creator and the wonder of his creation.

A friend told me this story: "When my daughter, Jen, started school I would drop her off at her baby-sitter on my way to work. The sitter lived about three blocks from the school. After a little while I found out from the teacher that Jen was late for school every day. I couldn't understand it. I dropped her off early, and she walked to school with the sitter's sons. They left the house in plenty of time to get there. When the sitter asked her boys if they knew why or how Jen was late for school so often, they commented, 'She walks so slow and looks at everything along the way. She stops and smells the flowers and touches things.' She just needed more time to walk so that she could enjoy God's creation!"[2]

Little children are filled with wonder when they observe the world in which they live. And in the face of that, they do not need to be told that they are little and powerless. They know it. Because they are little and powerless and, for the most part, trusting, they allow the creation to teach them about their loving Creator. Filled with wonder, they look and they listen. The mind of a small child is not yet filled with detailed information, responsibilities, or his or her own importance—so it's the heart, not the mind, that draws the child to what is important.

What happened to both Mary in the Bible and Jamie at summer camp that made them act as they did, ignoring the logic of the world about them? They had experienced the love of God. They were totally absorbed in his love, as it flooded their hearts; they saw their littleness and God's greatness. Dazzled, they turned their faces toward God, and he enveloped them in his tender love. Mary humbled herself, like a little child, and she saw in Jesus the kingdom of God. Jamie *was* a child, and his heart was already open to seeing God.

Like the disciples, we have fallen prey to logic. We are so busy with the knowledge of God that we have lost sight of what's important. That's why Jesus said that we need to become like little children. God touches our heart, and our perspective begins to change. Scripture says: "I will give you a new heart. . . . I will remove the heart of stone from your flesh and give you a heart of flesh" (Ezek. 36:26). In other words, our hearts will become tender toward God and toward our world. And—just as the words to the song from Andrew Lloyd

Webber's *Aspects of Love* say—"love changes everything."
Love touches us, and we are changed!

God reaches out to all of us. He calls us to surrender
all we know and open our hearts to his transforming
love. He knows that the ability of the small child to be
totally absorbed by something is what we need to recapture if we are to come to him wholeheartedly.

When we see our littleness in comparison to God's
greatness, then we will humble ourselves and become
like little children, welcoming the kingdom of God into
our lives. Taking a few minutes each day for the faithful practice of the prayer of love will help us get things
in perspective. It transforms us. Our pride and arro-
gance begin to melt away in the warm glow of God's
unconditional love as he draws us, his beloved children,
into the family circle of the Trinity.

In the prayer of silence, our tender, loving God holds
us close to his heart and immerses us in the mystery of
his love. The eyes of our heart will be opened, so that
we see the Lord who dwells within us. As we see God
for who he is, we see ourselves as we truly are—humble, precious, and beloved children of the Father.

9

You Are Precious

You are precious in my eyes, and honored, and I love you. . . . Fear not, for I am with you.

Isaiah 43:4–5 NOAB

For eighteen years my office was located in a large motel that was owned by Bill Volkman, the editor of the magazine for which I worked. Over the years Bill had had a weekly Bible study and/or prayer meeting for the motel staff, on company time. Virtually the only people who ever came were the housekeeping staff and occasionally someone from the front desk. All Christians, mostly women, these people were poor, and some were barely literate—either because of lack of education or because English was their second language.

One Wednesday it was my turn to lead the half-hour session—but I had completely forgotten. I was totally absorbed in preparing for the contemplative prayer retreat that would be held the next weekend at the motel. The phone rang, interrupting my work.

"Jan, this is Glenna. It's one o'clock. Are you coming to our prayer meeting?"

Oops!

"Oh, Glenna! I'm so sorry. I completely forgot! I'll be right there."

I stood staring at my messy desk for a moment, wondering what on earth I was going to share with them. I hadn't even thought about it. I'd prepared nothing!

Then, like a lightbulb flashing in my mind, the thought came: *Be honest with them. Tell them you didn't prepare and ask them if they would like you to share what you are going to do at the retreat this weekend.*

So that's what I did. I told them about the contemplative prayer retreat and what we would be doing. Then we read the verse from Isaiah that says: "You are precious in my eyes, and honored, and I love you. . . . Fear not, for I am with you" (Isa. 43:4–5 NOAB). I told them how much God longs for them to come and sit quietly in his presence, that they do not need to be afraid of what to say, for this is prayer without saying a word and God delights in our coming just to be with him.

Then Bill asked them if they would like to try sitting in silent prayer for five minutes. Enthusiastically they all said, "Yes!"

They quickly grasped that they could do this. They didn't need to have a lot of knowledge or pious phrases to come to God this way. They could truly come as they were and be accepted by him, because he could see their hearts were turned toward him.

From that day on, every time we met, we sat in silent prayer for five minutes. But before we did, someone would always ask, "Read that verse again—the one that says we are *precious.*"

Whether this verse is new to us or very familiar, it is still amazing! It is something we can never tire of hearing. Like the motel staff, the people in the small groups with whom I meet during my annual visit to Australia usually say the same thing: "Read that verse about how precious we are!"

Just as lovers never tire of being told, "I love you," we never tire of hearing God speaking directly, personally, and *particularly* to us, telling us how precious we are to him.

Whenever we come to the Lord, as a small child comes to a parent, he reveals the same marvelous, almost unbelievable truth—that we are the beloved of God. Zephaniah emphasizes this: "The LORD your God . . . will take great delight in you, he will quiet you with his love, he will rejoice over you with singing" (Zeph. 3:17 NIV).

Imagine! The Lord takes delight in *me!* He rejoices over *me* with singing! The great and awesome God of the universe is in love with *me,* and he calls *me* into his arms with an amazingly tender, gentle, all-encompassing love. My reasonable, logical mind tells me that this is sentimental drivel. But my heart tells me it's the truth. God truly does love me and can't wait, as the Jerusalem Bible translation of the same verse says, to renew me with his love, and "to dance with shouts of joy" for me!

The truth is that the living Christ Jesus dwells in our hearts, enlivening us with his Spirit and giving us his power to love the Father with his own love, as well as to love one another as he loves us. He takes great delight in us. If we will surrender ourselves to the security of his embrace, his love will quiet our busy minds and calm our clamoring thoughts. Surrounded and encircled by love, we will learn to rest in him.

When I think of the Trinity and how God loves us, surrounds us, and protects us, I am reminded of something I witnessed on a fishing trip in the southern Pacific. Some of the best game-fishing waters in the world are found a mile or two off the coast of New Zealand in the Pacific Ocean. The most sought-after fish are primarily marlin, weighing from two hundred to a thousand pounds each. Specially equipped boats, plus a lot of support, strength, time, and patience, are needed to catch and land one of these great fighting fish. I've been on a couple of game-fishing expeditions and, to me, the best part was being able to observe the marine life that lived at that distance from the coast. My favorite vantage point on the boat was the deck above the cabin, from which I could easily see deep into the clear blue-green water.

One day I lay on the deck and lazily watched as a school of dolphins swam and frolicked alongside our slowly moving boat. They would raise their sleek gray heads, watch our boat with alert button eyes, leap into the air as one, and then dive beneath the waves again. Each time the school broke the surface of the water, their slightly opened mouths made them look as if they were laughing, having the time of their lives! After a little while of watching them, something caught my attention. The next time they surfaced, I watched more closely. Right in the midst of this crowd of twenty or more adult dolphins was a tiny baby dolphin! He was laughing, leaping, and diving, completely encircled by the entire school, safely in the very middle of them! For perhaps fifteen minutes our joyful escort swam and played alongside us, finally diving as one and heading out to sea.

The care, the joy, and the love that was lavished on that tiny baby dolphin by those twenty or so huge animals makes me think of the inviting circle of the Trinity. Our God is the Rock in whom we find protection; the Cloud that sheltered the Israelites from the blazing sun; the Good Shepherd who leads his sheep by still waters, who finds the lost and enfolds them in his arms close to his heart; the Christ in whom we are hid and who dwells in our hearts.

93

Our tender, loving God reveals his heart to us in the words of Jesus. He speaks to Jerusalem of his longing to gather her people "as a hen gathers her chicks under her wings." All too often we respond just as Jesus said the people of Jerusalem did: "But you were not willing" (Luke 13:34 NIV).

Why are we unwilling to respond? We are deathly afraid of being known by God; we are afraid of what it will cost us, and, most of all, we fear intimacy with God because we believe, falsely, that if we get close to him, he will tell us something we don't want to hear.

When I was in Australia in 1997, Christians there were asking each other a strange question: "If Jesus returned today, what do you think he would say to the church?"

The surprising answer was, simply, "I love you."

Why are we surprised by the answer? Because, for most of us, the answer that immediately comes to mind is something like: He'd tell us how bad we are!

Why does our focus tend to be on how much we fall short, on how bad we are, instead of on how good and wonderful and loving God is? Perhaps few who casually mouthed these words grasped how true they were—that they were expressing a profound truth. To love and be loved and to give birth to love is our destiny. The gospel is the good news of God's unconditional love for us. Our birthright is to be like God, who is love. All we have to do is believe him. Why, then, don't we? One of the reasons is, of course, that we focus on how much we fall short. Instead, we need to *practice* being the beloved.

There is a Scripture that begins with the words, "The eyes of the LORD move to and fro throughout the earth" (2 Chron. 16:9). Once again, when we hear that God is watching us, our first thought is something like: *He's out to catch me doing something wrong!* We think God is like Santa, checking to see if we've been naughty or nice. But could it be that his eyes are on us because he

94

loves us so much *he can't take his eyes off us?* You know how lovers are. They can't get enough of looking at the one they love. He is the Lover, and we are the object of his love.

On the farm, my dad's mount was a beautiful Arab mare. From time to time, she gave birth to an exquisite foal. Within a few hours of its birth, Dad would begin to work with the new foal. Bringing the mare and her precious newborn into the corral, Dad would talk quietly to them, as he gradually approached them. Each day, for an hour or so, he would do this. I don't remember how many days it took, but I do remember that I loved to stand at the fence, watching and listening.

Eventually the gangly legged little creature stopped bolting to the far side of its mother whenever my father got close. The whole time he was in the corral Dad would be talking softly, reaching out his hand, never approaching any closer than the mare and her foal allowed. Gradually it became apparent, from his pricked ears and calm eyes, that the little horse was listening to the reassuring sound of my dad's voice. Days of patient talking, coaxing, and just being with them would eventually pay off. The little horse would finally allow itself to be touched, stroked, and fondled without bolting away with its ears back and its tail and hoofs flying.

My dad's words were always softly spoken words of encouragement: "There, there, you little beauty. That's the way. Just come to me. I'm not going to hurt you. Good, good. Come to me, now. Just relax. Ah, you're beautiful. Ah, good foal."

Over and over he would say the same words, keeping up a constant stream of low, encouraging dialogue. No matter how his pupil responded, my father always spoke with quiet, gentle reassurance and praise.

The toughest step was always when, for the first time—as he talked softly and stroked the foal's mane—he cautiously dropped a light rope across its neck. Usually the pretty little creature's nostrils would flare, its ears would flatten, its eyes would almost pop out, and it would stamp in outrage and bolt away, flinging its head till the rope fell off. Shortly afterward, when the relationship was reestablished, Dad would throw the rope over the foal's neck again. Over and over the scene was repeated, each time the foal reacting with outrage. Finally, the foal calmed down, accepted the light weight of the rope, and eventually ignored it.

After several months, a rope-halter was accepted and, after some more time, my dad and the little horse walked together slowly around the dusty yard. With his head proudly arched, the foal's gait was perfectly in step with my father's. Watching them was a joy, and as they came close to where I stood, I could hear my dad's gentle words of praise and approval.

With his constant, quiet presence, my father won the trust and confidence of the young horse. After that, when they walked together, sometimes the horse led the way, accompanied by just a few of my dad's affirming words.

I see God working with similar purpose, love, and patience with us, gently encouraging us as we make choices in our lives. Like the foal, we tend to be skittish and unsure at first. Sadly, our focus is so often on where we have failed that we forget that his grace is greater than all our shortcomings. Often our view of God comes directly from a tyrannical teacher or parent who we felt was impossible to please.

Even though the Scriptures are filled with affirmations of us, these are not the passages that spring to mind. So, even when we read it in the Bible, we can't quite believe that God loves us unconditionally and that he patiently understands when we make mistakes. We are so busy berating ourselves that we don't hear the quiet, gentle voice of love speaking to us deep in our spirit, saying, "There, there, my precious. That's the way. Just come to me."

Coming to him, coming home to where we belong, to nestle in his arms, close to his heart, is our destiny. The Lord who dwells within us waits for us to calm down, to be still and quiet, to respond to his call. He wants to be precious to us. He waits for us to make prayer, especially silent prayer, a regular part of our lives.

God is prepared to work with us, gently going through the same lessons over and over again. Throughout each experience, his loving words of encouragement are being whispered to us. As our trust in him deepens, we will begin to walk with confidence, knowing that our loving God goes with us, delighting in every step we take. As we venture onto a new path, if we listen closely, we will eventually hear his gentle words echoing in our heart, "Ah, yes, my precious one. This is the way, walk in it."

10

Under His Wings

How often I have longed to gather your children together,
as a hen gathers her chicks *under her wings*.

Luke 13:34 NIV

Growing up on a farm, my brother and sister and I all
had daily chores. Throughout my childhood the one
chore I didn't have to be told to do was taking care of
our free-range hens. I loved the daily search for eggs—
hens don't always lay in the boxes that we provide for
them—and the eager gathering of the hens around me
when I turned up with their ration of grain.

We had Rhode Island Reds, black Orpingtons, and
white leghorns. The white leghorns had white feathers
and long yellow legs. They were shrill, skinny, and
crabby. The Rhode Island Reds were bigger, had beautiful russet-colored feathers, bright, alert eyes, and quiet
dispositions.

To me, the prettiest and calmest birds were the black
Orpingtons. They were plump black hens with short
gray legs. I learned that if I sat on the ground with my

skirt spread over my knees, kept very still, and talked softly, one of them would come and sit in my lap. Eyeing me all the time, the hen would caw and croon to me as I quietly talked or sang, all the while stroking her red comb and her silky black feathers, which glowed with purple, green, and gold rainbows in the sunlight.

Over the years, I named all the hens—but my favorite was a big black Orpington called Esmeralda. These large, calm hens made the best mothers. Unlike some of the other breeds, they would sit on a handful of eggs, unperturbed by whatever was going on around them. As soon as Esmeralda had hatched and raised a clutch of chickens, I would find her sitting on a few eggs making her special "clucky" sound again. I was always overjoyed, as this meant that in a few weeks we would have more tiny chicks to watch over.

Esmeralda sat low in the hatching nest, her wings outspread, touching the straw. With eyes half-closed, she clucked away quietly to herself. All the feathers from her underside had been removed as she had lined the nest with them. Morning and night I went quietly into her fox-proof enclosure and slid my hand under her spread-out feathers to check if any eggs were hatched. It was so warm and secure under those wings. Some of the other hens pecked at my hand if I did that—but not Esmeralda. She trusted me!

My dad always knew when the incubation period was up. He would tell me, "Today you will probably find a chick has hatched." I entered into the enclosure as usual, quietly and cautiously approached the hatching nest, and, as I did so, I caught Esmeralda's sharp eye watching me. The pitch of her quiet clucking was raised momentarily, warning me. Ha! There *was* a chick hatched. The watchful eye and the different sounds told me so.

Very slowly I slipped my hand under her feathers, and out peeked the bold little face of a newborn chick, only to quickly disappear back into the warmth and safety of those outstretched wings. Esmeralda usually raised her wings a little, wiggled herself into position, crooned a little, and then settled back down again. I sat there, on the ground in front of the hatching nest, fascinated, until someone from the house called me to come in.

As the eggs hatched, this scene was repeated many times. Esmeralda was to live a long life, continuing to raise new clutches of chicks.

I love the picture that springs to my mind when I read the words of Jesus: "Jerusalem, Jerusalem . . . how often I have longed to gather your children together, as a hen gathers her chicks *under her wings*" (Luke 13:34 NIV).

A firefighter tells of walking with a colleague through a forest after a fire. Blackened trees stand like sentinels over a silent landscape. There are no leaves left to rustle in the slight breeze. There are no birds in the trees, no animals skittering around in the nonexistent undergrowth. Little spirals of gray smoke rise here and there. The firefighters' heavy protective boots cause little puffs of ash to rise as they walk past the charred remains of animals and birds, either on the forest floor or still clinging to blackened branches. They come to a clearing and are confronted by a stark brick chimney—all that is left of a house. Tucked against the trunk of a nearby tree is the burned carcass of a hen. While his buddy watches, the firefighter nonchalantly moves the remains with the toe of his boot—and they are both startled when three tiny yellow chicks run out! The mother's body and feathers had totally insulated them from the deadly fire.

We are being drawn to God by his great love for us. He waits for us, peering into the distance, looking for us to turn around, just as the loving father did in the prodigal son story. He calls us home as surely as we call our small children when they are outside playing—and as surely as the mother hen calls her chicks to the safety and shelter of her wings. We are more precious to God than we can imagine.

We desperately need to recapture the boldness of the small, much-loved child and "boldly approach the throne of our gracious God" (Heb. 4:16 NEB).

In the early '90s my brother's first grandchild was born. Thomas came into the world with big blue eyes and blond curls and a bevy of adoring family eagerly awaiting his arrival. He had a full set of great-grandparents and grandparents, as well as aunts, uncles, and many other extended family members. Everyone thought that he was wonderful—and he knew it. From his first few weeks on, everywhere he went, he looked people full in the face with a broad toothless smile, fully expecting a smile in return. If people looked at him, they couldn't help but respond to his enthusiasm for life. Thomas was not afraid of rejection. He'd never experienced it, so he didn't expect it. His world was a welcoming, safe, and loving place.

Over and over again, whenever God sent a messenger to earth to tell us of his loving action on our behalf, the first words spoken were "Don't be afraid." Yet we remain afraid and unsure of his loving intention toward us.

As we gather at church or in our fellowship groups, what is the topic of our conversation? How much we are loved? How much the Lord wants a relationship with us? How approachable he is? How much he longs to just "hang out" with us? How, when we become very still and quiet, we will become aware of his whispered words of love to us?

Even if these things are our personal experience, we are often afraid to talk about such things. We stick to safe topics—trivia, books we are reading, local news, or sports. Occasionally we'll talk about who needs prayer. But things of life-and-death importance are rarely shared! We don't discuss what makes real our relationship with Jesus. We don't reveal the emptiness in our hearts. We don't talk about how we can be comforted in God's presence like a small child in the arms of a parent.

Years ago I drove to a Christian conference with a woman who had just buried her brain-damaged infant. The child had died a few days earlier after getting an infection in the hospital. Even though the child's chances of a life with any quality to it had been minimal, this grieving mother was distraught. The two-day conference was crammed full from early morning until late at night with long messages from a couple of speakers, plus announcements, rousing music, opening and closing prayers, and meal blessings from an efficient emcee who hurried everyone off to their rushed meals and back for the next session—all very wonderful but hardly the atmosphere for someone who was deeply hurting.

There was not a moment, absolutely no opportunity, throughout this conference for the poor woman to share her pain and grief with the Christian community gathered there and to be comforted by them. I wonder how many of our churches make the same mistake? How many people come in pain and leave empty-handed because there was no opportunity, no moment, for them to share their pain and be comforted? The scheduled, structured program leaves no room for it. And how often do we get the feeling that the program is more important than anything else? How often am I, as a member of a church, guilty of being too busy to bother with people in need of comfort?

Unless we as individuals allow ourselves to be healed and made whole by our loving Creator, we will not be sensitive to the needs of others. Most of us are just a walking bundle of needs, totally wrapped up in our own little world. Churches and fellowship groups are made up of hurting, damaged people, most of whom are desperately in need of God's healing touch. Perhaps, because of this, church is not always the best place to go when we are hurting. So where can we go?

We can come home. We can turn within to the Lord, who is quietly waiting in our hearts, and, without words, we can immerse ourselves in his great love for us.

Jesus told us that his people would be known by their love for one another (John 13:35). But, before we can love each other, we have to know without a shadow of doubt—as my niece's little son Thomas knew—that we are loved unconditionally.

Hanging out the window of a Dover-bound train at London's Victoria station, Corrie ten Boom was returning to Europe after a tour of English churches in the '70s. As the train pulled away, she spoke these memorable words to a little huddle of black-robed young clerics who had come to see her off: "Remember, don't wrestle, nestle!"

God's sheltering wings are spread out, inviting each one of us to come to him and not be afraid. He calls us home to him, into his everlasting arms—for love, for healing, for comfort, and for rest. Let's not be like the people who "were not willing." Let's respond to God's call. Let's come into the silence of the cloud of unknowing, nestle into the shelter of those outstretched wings, and allow him to make us whole.

II

Opening the Door

Behold, I stand at the door and knock; if anyone hears My voice and *opens the door*, I will come in.

Revelation 3:20

Do you remember when you first fell in love? Remember how you and your lover couldn't wait to be together, how long each moment was when you were apart? Remember how quickly you responded when you heard that beloved voice and how you felt when you saw that beloved face? Remember how you hung on every word, how you couldn't wait to talk about every little thing, how you never seemed to run out of things to share? Remember how much fun, how magical everything was that you did together, no matter how ordinary and mundane?

Do you remember feeling that this wonderful romance would never become old—it would, could, never end? You would never sit across the table from each other at a restaurant bored out of your mind with nothing to say to each other. Remember how you couldn't wait to go home and make love and how you couldn't understand why other married couples ignored each other? Remember being puzzled when you saw a couple sitting together staring into space instead of at each other or walking together and not even holding hands? Did you ever wonder why so many people allow their love to grow cold, living as polite strangers under the same roof?

Many of us do remember when we first fell in love but, for many, our "great love relationship" deteriorated into "two polite strangers" or no longer exists as a relationship at all. Nurturing that first glow of love so that it grows into a mature, vibrant, life-giving relationship takes a great deal of time, energy, and sacrifice. It involves taking enormous risks, continually going the extra mile, and constantly opening ourselves up when our feelings scream at us to withdraw and shut ourselves away.

We know that a living, loving relationship takes a day-by-day commitment to self-sacrifice by both parties, but most of us want it anyway, knowing that it's vital for a happy life. But we don't seem to realize that the same is true of our spiritual life.

Our Creator longs for each one of us to commit to a love relationship with him. He is waiting for us. "Can you not see Him waiting for you?" is the way the author of *The Cloud of Unknowing* puts it.[1]

And, can't you? Don't you see all the little "love notes" the Lord is constantly leaving you, trying to entice you into responding to his love? Do you look at a sunrise or a sunset dispassionately? Do you ignore the fresh flowers in the vase, the newly opened spring flowers, the just-hatched butterflies drying their wings on a tree trunk as you rush past on your daily walk in the woods? Do you take for granted a near miss in the evening rush-hour traffic, the flash of a reminder to get a birthday gift for a loved one, the health scare that turns out to be nothing to worry about? Even when we walk through the valley of the shadow of death—a horrible accident that turns our world upside down; the health scare that is our worst fear realized—God's light and love filter through, giving us glimpses of his caring presence with us.

Is it just possible that God is quietly but constantly intervening in our lives in ways that we can barely perceive? He wants us to know that he loves us passionately and hopes that perhaps one day we will return his love.

I married very young, and I was very much in love with my husband. Because of what I saw in my parents' marriage, when I fell in love, I naturally assumed that it would be a lifetime, ever-growing love like they had.

Throughout my marriage—which lasted just under six years before my husband's death—I wrote love notes to him and hid them everywhere. He found notes in his sock drawer and his underwear drawer, in the pocket of his overalls, in his toolbox, in the glove box, in his lunch box between his sandwiches, under his pillow, in his ammunition or tackle box (he loved to hunt and fish), and even on the steering wheel of the car as he left for work. I wasn't doing it to woo him, because the love was mutual. I did it because I couldn't tell or show him enough how special and wonderful and cherished he was.

This simple human example is only a taste of how the Lord is with us. I see the Scriptures and the creation filled to overflowing with God's longing for a relationship with us. Can't you?

He offers himself as an ever-willing self-sacrifice, as our exciting first love, as a comforting good companion, as an intimate lifelong friend. He is always there, never leaving or forsaking us. He's vitally interested in us and is never too busy to listen to us. Constantly available for intimate communion, he speaks in a gentle whisper, telling us over and over how precious we are to him.

We don't notice God's love notes because we are so busy with our own thoughts and plans. He's waiting for us to turn to him and respond to him. Yes, he is the transcendent God, sitting at the controls of the universe. But he's also an immanent and personal God who came in human flesh, in Jesus, and made his home in first-century Palestine. He wants, in this twenty-first century, to make his home in human flesh again, within us.

If we are honest, we will admit to being just a little leery of a God who wants to get *that* close. We prefer to come to God with a laundry list of things to ask for, with a book to read, a question to ponder, or a Scripture about which we want enlightenment. We don't come to God for *himself*—we come for what we can get out of him. We come to *get*, not just to *be*.

Being is hard. We find it equally hard to *be* with our human spouse, with our children, with our parents, or with our friends. We even find it hard to just *be* with ourselves. We have to have something to *do*, to say, to listen to, or to think about. God made us to love and be loved and to *enjoy* him, as the Westminster Catechism says: "... to glorify God and to enjoy Him for ever."[2] But we have to admit that glorifying God and enjoying him seem almost impossible for us.

The saints of the past write of a passionate relationship with the Lord, but we find it hard to believe that God wants such a relationship with us. After all, we are not saints. It seldom occurs to us that an intimate relationship with the Lord is possible, so we don't even ask for it—"You do not have because you do not ask" (James 4:2). We spend so much time in our heads—studying and dissecting the Scriptures and reading books about them and about God—that there is very little time left for the God who dwells in our hearts.

It's as if we invited our Lover God into our home, and before we even welcome him, we leave him sitting in the family room, waiting for us to come to him. At the same time, we are sitting at the kitchen table, head down, diligently studying the Scriptures *about* him!

Jesus challenged his hearers with these words: "You *search the Scriptures,* because you think that in them you have eternal life . . . and you are unwilling to come to Me so that you may have life" (John 5:39–40). And his words carry the same challenge to us today! He is calling us to come home to him.

David Watson of York—a charismatic Anglican evangelist who led the renewal movement in England in the '70s—asked, "Do we have the Father, Son, and Holy *Scriptures* as our Trinity?"[3] He challenged Christians to look up from their study of the Word and *see* the Lord, the *Living Word,* who is waiting for them to come to him for life!

I know that God has called us to intimacy, and I love that he has. But I still forget. I'm as guilty as anyone— I too hold back from coming to him. I find myself looking for things to do to avoid my times of centering prayer. I tell others about the importance and power of silent prayer, but there are times when I allow everything else to take precedence over it in my life.

The Song of Songs paints a poignant picture for us to ponder:

> I sleep, but my heart is awake.
> I hear my Beloved knocking.
> "Open to me . . . my love, my dove, my perfect one."
> .   .   .   .
> I have taken off my tunic,
> am I to put it on again?

I have washed my feet,
am I to dirty them again?"

Song of Songs 5:2–3 JB

What makes us respond like that? Why do we put off a wholehearted giving of ourselves to the Lord? The Song of Songs continues: "I rose to open to my Beloved . . . but I did not find him" (vv. 5–6 JB).

Jesus comes knocking on the door of our heart, but, instead of rushing to open it, we are busy playing Martha. He calls on us to be like Mary—to choose the "better part" for at least a few minutes each day. But, like the foolish lover in the Song of Songs, we are in no hurry to let go of our self-centered agenda and open the door.

The Lord calls on us to dare to throw ourselves into his arms, to surrender ourselves to him, to be completely open and "naked" in his presence—to give up all our cover and just be his. We surrender the need to keep secrets from the Lord (as if that were possible!). We acknowledge our failure to love as he loves, and we boldly open the pages of our lives. Then we find that our deep-seated psychic wounds are being healed.

The surprising thing is that, as we loosen the grip that our false self has on us, we will care less and less about what other people think. We will gradually become our true selves, more transparent to others and more open to see ourselves as the wonderful, beautiful, uniquely made individuals that we are. We will have no qualms when we see our need to "strip, spoil and utterly unclothe [our] self-awareness of everything," so that we might be "newly clothed in the gracious stark experience of God," as the author of *The Cloud* says.[4]

109

In human marriage, without the experience of union with one's spouse, one is living a lie; the marriage is a fraud—so too in our love relationship with the Lord.

Speaking to a church filled with people who are satisfied with their lukewarm relationship with him, the Lord says: "Behold, I stand at the door and knock; if any one hears My voice and *opens the door,* I will come in" (Rev. 3:20). He truly is standing at the door of our heart, knocking. Is our response like the words of an old song, "I hear you knocking, but you can't come in"?

Why do we turn a deaf ear to that knocking? Probably because opening the door of our heart to intimacy with the Lord is too scary for us. Like a skittish bride who continues to party with her friends, putting off for as long as possible the time of being all alone with her new husband, we put off responding to the knocking on the door of our hearts.

Let's get into the habit of responding to the Bridegroom. Let's be wiser than the lover in the Song of Songs. Let's return to our "first love." Let's respond quickly, open the door of our hearts, and give ourselves to him in love. Patiently the Lord is waiting for us to turn within, where he dwells.

Can you not see him waiting for you?

12

Do Not Be Afraid ... You Are Mine

Do not be afraid, for I have redeemed you; I have called
you by name, *you are mine.*

Isaiah 43:1 JB

It was the week before Christmas 1979—my first Christmas in the United States. I had been in Illinois just a month. We had unpacked all the boxes, and all the furniture we brought with us from England was in place. The biting cold weather, culture shock (I had spent the previous six years in England), and a horrid eleven-year marriage all had me feeling off balance, out of my depth, and anything but at home.

But my husband wanted to fill the empty spaces in the living areas of our new home as quickly as possible, so we were shopping for furniture. I hate to shop at the best of times, so I dejectedly trotted around the store after him while he made his selections. Passive and depressed, I was like a cork tossed by the sea, drifting wherever time and tide took me.

111

I had the vague hope that a new place—a new country, no less—would have sufficient magic to perform a miracle in our lives and give us a new start in our marriage. But I was feeling helpless and almost hopeless. *Perhaps,* I thought, *God will intervene and make everything right.*

A few days later, as I tried to settle into this strange new world, I was halfheartedly doing a little Christmas gift shopping, despite the demands of a full-time job and elaborate holiday cooking requirements. During the last week before Christmas I had shopped for all the traditional English holiday fare—which was no easy task in a non-English culture. Then, just as it was getting dark on Christmas Eve, I realized suddenly that I had no Christmas gift for my husband. Frantically, I ran from shopping mall to shopping mall, only to find most of the gift shops already closed. Finally, I went home, exhausted, dejected. I had no gift, no card.

Christmas morning dawned. There was no Christmas tree in our new house. What was the point of a Christmas tree—which we were accustomed to buying and decorating on Christmas Eve before going to church at midnight—when no one would be there but the two of us? All our family and friends were on other continents or on the West Coast. We had none of the usual Christmas trappings. The air in the house was chilly, and I couldn't even find any Christmas music on the unfamiliar radio stations.

At breakfast, I felt as if we were strangers as I faced my husband across the table. I was horrified when he produced a gift-wrapped package. Only once in eleven years had he given me a Christmas gift. I hadn't expected to have my lack shown up in this way. I opened the gift and was surprised to find it was something I had wanted for some time that I wasn't even aware he knew about. Thoroughly miserable now, I numbly thanked him.

With an incredible sinking feeling, I looked into his face and said, "I didn't get you anything. I was afraid." Now it was his turn to be horrified.

"What do you mean, you didn't get me anything—you were afraid!?"

Backed into a corner, I defended myself: "I mean that I didn't get you anything, because I didn't know what you wanted. And I was afraid to spend any more money!"

He sat and looked at me for the longest time, and then he put his head in his hands and began to cry. He didn't say anything. He just sat there and cried. And my heart sank. I didn't know what to do.

I set out all the carefully purchased and prepared traditional food for the occasion. Then we went to church and went through the motions, but it was a joyless holiday.

Even after eleven years, I didn't really know this man I was married to. I had no idea what he was thinking— or even what his hopes and dreams were. But I knew that my worst fear was about to be realized. This was going to be a new beginning for our marriage all right. It spelled its end. The death knell had just been sounded. And, like a rabbit caught in the headlights of a car, my fear immobilized me. I could do nothing. I could say nothing.

We were divorced a little over a year later, and I was left to deal with all my fears the only way I could— through living one day at a time and by focusing on the One who casts out fear (see 1 John 4:18).

Even now, sometimes I forget and allow my fears to stop me from facing the truth about myself, or about another person or a situation I am in. When I do that, I stop God from blessing me.

As timid "much afraids," we human beings allow our irrational fears to stop us from expressing our feelings to others—expressions of thanks, appreciation, joy, and love. Those same fears will also stop us from entering into an intimate, loving relationship with God.

Australian aboriginal babies are born with a song of welcome echoing in their ears. The mother's closest female relatives gather, and throughout the birth process they sing of their love for the newborn. Every baby is looked on as a precious gift from the Great Spirit to the whole community and as a special gift to the family. They sing of how each family member is eagerly awaiting the baby's arrival, of their wish for his safe journey from his spiritual home, of how glad they are that the child has joined them at last, and of his good and joyful future with them.

Just like the aboriginal baby, each one of us is born with a song of welcome echoing in our ears. Our loving God sings a song to us, telling us, "Do not be afraid. . . . I have called you by name, *you are mine*" (Isa. 43:1 JB). This song is sung to us from the beginning and throughout our lives—but we are not listening, for we are tuned in to another song, a siren song that draws us away from God.

The siren song draws us to a world filled with glittering and tantalizing images, and we, with the encouragement of our unwitting parents, do our best to fit in, to conform. Before we know it, we believe that a fairytale life can be ours. Barely into adolescence, we can't wait to rush into an intimate relationship and to say to another human being, "You are mine, and I am yours." We quickly discover that, like fire, sexuality is a good servant but a bad master. It wounds us and wreaks havoc in our lives. Why did God create us with this two-edged sword of bane and blessing? And what does it have to do with prayer? It has everything to do with prayer, because both prayer and sexuality are integral to our most important and intimate relationships.

Human sexuality is at the forefront of our lives—determining and defining our personality, our status in society, our role in the church, and our work both in the home and in the business world. It's something we can't hide from, because the most obvious thing about a person is his or her sex.

Deep within us we all sense the need to be close to someone we love—closer than breathing, actually. We desire to be inside someone or to have someone inside of us—we feel a need to be in union with the loved one. But we soon discover that even making love doesn't satisfy those feelings of need for very long. We just don't seem to be able to get filled up to our satisfaction. The reason is simple. Our ultimate destiny is to hear God's song of love, respond to him, and be filled up with him.

The Lord created humanity in his image, but he created us incomplete—with a gnawing hunger and emptiness that needs to be filled. One writer calls that hunger a God-shaped space, a space that can be filled only by God.

At birth we emerge into this world screaming our outrage at our sense of incompleteness, longing to be whole. The arts, especially music—whether classical, pop, country, folk, blues, jazz, or rock—express our melancholy search for fulfillment and love.

We are afraid that we won't find someone to share our lives with, so, as time goes by, our search becomes more frantic. Our family and our peers put pressure on us to give up our single status. But no one tells us—perhaps because they don't know themselves—how vital it is that our significant other be someone we love enough to die for. They don't tell us that there is a vast difference between a fleeting attraction that will not withstand the rigors of a lifetime relationship and a deep abiding love that will.

115

While in my early twenties, I met a very old, very charming, very successful woman. She laughingly told me that she had never married because she had never met a man she couldn't live without! She said, "When I was a young woman on my way to university, my dad took me aside and said, 'Do as you please, my dear, but don't marry unless you meet a man you can't live without.' And I never did! And I've never regretted it!"

Of course, I didn't follow her example! When I married for the second time, I foolishly did it without making a wholehearted, to-die-for commitment. I believe that the kind of love that is needed to sustain marriage for a lifetime is sacrificial—it's a love that is prepared to die for the other.

Whether we care to admit it or not, the intimacy and openness of human sexuality gives us a graphic picture of what our relationship with God is intended to be. The openness, the nakedness, the sacrifice of one's time, the abandonment of self for the spouse's happiness are all essential components of a living love relationship. They are a necessary part of our union with God, which is our destiny and has been from the beginning. Without union with God, we are empty, lonely, and unfulfilled.

Because of his desire for this intimate union with each person—"nearer than hands and feet," one poet says[1]—the picture of sexual union is probably the closest we can come to describe intimacy with God.

Whether or not we find our human one true love, God continues to call and woo us—his bride—into relationship with him. Even if we are in the deepest pits of a horrible human relationship or in the darkness of an addiction, he still calls us to the one union that will fill our every desire—union with him, the One in whose image we were created and who alone knows the exact shape of our incompleteness.

116

Whenever we enter into an intimate relationship with another person—whether it's by a church wedding with all the trimmings or a casual one-night stand—the experience usually only highlights the depth of our need. Almost at once we find that we are right back to that gnawing emptiness again. Marriage is all too often plagued by self-centeredness rather than other-centeredness, with neither spouse ever experiencing a sense of union of body, soul, and spirit.

We are made to love—to love other human beings, including our human spouse, and to love God, our heavenly Spouse. God knows us and calls us by name. He knows our heart's desires. He tells us that we are precious and he loves us. And despite our hectic rush to find love elsewhere, he continues to remind us that we are his beloved.

Listen to the song our Lover has written to us in the Song of Songs. Listen as if it were the voice of the Lord speaking directly to your heart, and let his love change you.

> How beautiful you are, my Beloved,
> How beautiful you are!
> Your eyes are doves.
>
> As a lily among the thistles,
> so is my love among the maidens.
>
> You are wholly beautiful, my love,
> and without blemish.
>
> You ravish my heart
> with a single one of your glances.
>
> How beautiful you are,
> how charming, my love, my delight!

117

Set me like a seal on your heart,
like a seal on your arm.

Song of Songs 1:15; 2:2; 4:7,
9; 7:6; 8:6 JB

Please read the rest of this seldom-read book, seeing yourself as the bride, and practice being the beloved. Notice how the bride responds with similar words to the bridegroom. This is a tender, loving exchange.

We belong to God. We were made for him. "Do not be afraid, for I have redeemed you; I have called you by name, *you are mine*" is a song we were all created to hear. Made in his image, made in his likeness, we are made for love and to be love.

Through the prayer of love, we give ourselves to God in silent adoration. This is not a solemn silence, like that surrounding a Good Friday service. It's a joyous silence, like that enveloping us as we lie together with a beloved spouse after making love. As we turn our faces toward him, responding with the words of the bride in the Song of Songs: "My Beloved is mine and I am his" (2:16 JB), he fills us with his love, as he originally intended.

13

Like a Weaned Child

Surely I have composed and quieted my soul;
Like a weaned child rests against his mother,
My soul is like a weaned child within me.

Psalm 131:2

The prayer of silence is countercultural. In it we become like little children. We humble ourselves, setting aside all our human needs, putting our God first. We forget all we know, we surrender all our rights to speak and to be heard, and we sit in silence, both within and without. Not only do we not speak, but we do not continually think pious thoughts about God during the prayer. Rather, we compose and quiet our souls and remain completely silent. We come without an agenda. That's why the words in Psalm 131 are so appropriate. "O LORD, my heart is not proud, nor my eyes haughty; nor do I involve myself in great matters, or in things too difficult for me. Surely I have composed and quieted my soul; like a weaned child rests against his mother, my soul is like a weaned child within me" (vv. 1–2). A weaned child?

119

What in the world does that mean? What's so special about a weaned child?

Any mother will tell you that before a child is weaned, when he climbs onto her lap, *the child has an agenda.* He is coming to her with a specific purpose—to be fed. However, after the child is weaned, he will come to sit on the mother's lap just to be there, not to be fed. The child is coming to be with the mother, to be held, to feel close, to simply enjoy being with her.

In contemplative prayer, God calls us to come to him like a weaned child—*without an agenda.* He calls us to be still, to come not to talk or to be taught. We turn within, lay aside our thoughts, and go beyond thoughts, words, and emotions. We open our hearts—our whole being—to God.

We come to this prayer to give ourselves to God in love, to give ourselves as a gift to the Beloved. As much as we are able, we come to him without any ulterior motive— even any *good* motives. We come without words of praise or petition or penitence; those are for another time.

Our culture is focused on time management, on getting value for money. We are trained to think in terms of measurable results. So, whenever we do something, we always want to get the biggest bang for our buck. Most of us are overextended. Family, friends, work, recreation, sleep, home, church, all demand more of our time than we have. We have to juggle constantly to keep up and to stay sane. Why add the prayer of silence to our busy lives if it gets us nothing?

While there are no measurable results to contemplative prayer, it is not fruitless. As any farmer or orchardist will tell you, fruit is not instantaneous. It takes time, nurture, and patience. If you are faithful to the practice, there will be fruit. You may not be aware of it at first, but before long your friends and family will see that you have changed.

It's important to begin the prayer of silence expecting nothing. You are not listening for the Lord to speak, so don't expect to hear anything. And don't expect to feel anything. You are coming to the Lord just to *be*. But don't think that you can sit in the Lord's presence in silence day after day and not be changed!

Remember the story of Moses? After forty days on the mountaintop with God, he was so changed and his face glowed so much that the people were afraid and he had to cover his face with a veil! (see Exod. 34:30–35). After a little while you will have an inner glow that you can't hide. You will begin to reflect the light of Christ in a new way. You may not see the change, but just as we appreciate the light of a lamp as night approaches, people will be blessed by the change in you. Trust the Lord. Entrust yourself to him. Let him take care of the outcome.

For those of us who like to talk (doesn't everybody?), the thought of being silent before God is a challenge, especially if we've just discovered that the God we've so long sought to please actually desires an intimate relationship with us. Why, then, *silence*? Why, if I'm one with the Lord, do I need to pray at all? Isn't he, as one poet says, "closer than breathing"?[1] Aren't we in constant communication? Or, if I want to pray, why can't I just come to prayer and chatter my head off if that's what I've always done?

When I was a chatterbox teenager, my mother told me: "Conversation is like a game of tennis. You hit the ball over the net, and the other person is supposed to hit it back. The other player doesn't grab the ball and run away with it or start playing a game alone in the corner of the court. That would end the game. That's no fun! You have to pause and listen if you want people to be friends with you. You have to hit the ball back and let them have a turn!"

121

Many of us have never learned this most basic rule of conversation. Too often this is how we communicate with God. We say our piece and then we rush off to the next thing. In the prayer of love, the prayer of *silence*, the point is not even about listening, it's about being completely still and quiet, both *without* and *within*.

For some people, to suggest being silent in God's presence is close to heresy. "Doesn't the Scripture say that we have the mind of Christ? If so, then our thoughts are good! Where does the Scripture say to be silent? That sounds weird and unscriptural to me!" For others it sounds too much like legalism or new age.

In the Protestant evangelical world, we have many misconceptions about unfamiliar religious practices. We are often reluctant to change those misconceptions, because we tend to be afraid of the unfamiliar. One of those unfamiliar religious practices is contemplative prayer. Instead of facing the fear head-on, going to the source and getting to know about it, we tend to go into a huddle with other "much afraids" and do nothing.

As a very tiny child, I was afraid of the dark and would do anything to persuade my parents to leave a small lamp burning in my room (which they did). Even so, I often woke them with my squeals of terror. My dad would come into the room with a lantern and, holding his sobbing child in one arm, he would shine the light into every corner of the room—under the bed, in the wardrobe, behind the curtains—until I had seen there was nothing to fear.

We can truly trust God to protect and lead us in our search for truth and in our desire for depth in our religious life. Since, clearly, he hasn't given us a spirit that makes us a slave to fear (Rom. 8:15), there's no reason to stand back, afraid to even *listen* to how Christians from different traditions worship God. Silent prayer has been a practice in the church for a very long time. It got

122

buried during the upheaval of the Reformation. However, the practice did not die out completely; it continued in some monastic communities. In this generation, it is being discovered anew by many, both lay and clergy people.[2]

Unfortunately, there are some who think that contemplative prayer is only for the spiritually "elite." And, for others, silent prayer seems to be an oxymoron: "How can you pray if you don't *say* anything?"

Often, as I prepare to lead a contemplative prayer retreat—with an advertised schedule that includes twenty-minute "contemplative sitting" times—someone will explain his or her not attending by saying something like, "I don't think I could sit for twenty minutes of silent prayer or even ten minutes! I'd be uncomfortable. There's just too much going on in my head and in my life to do that. Maybe someday, when my life settles down, it would make more sense for me."

And it is true that in our busy, noisy culture, silence is something with which few are comfortable. In most cases, though, we find that as we sit in the Lord's presence in communion with others, the discomfort gives way to a surprising peacefulness, and the time goes faster than we could have ever imagined.

A prayer retreat is a time to *practice* the prayer of silence. It gives us some space in which to get used to the silence. Everyone who comes is a beginner, no matter how long they've been doing it. There are no experts!

In addition to encouraging us to be like a weaned child, Psalm 131 says, "my heart is not proud . . . nor do I involve myself in great matters" (v. 1). The heart of the contemplative is like the heart of Mary of Bethany. She was content to sit at Jesus' feet and adore him. She didn't have to discuss, talk, or analyze. She was content to *be*. How hard it is for us to be silent—to let go of all that we know. We love to discuss "great matters"; we love our knowledge. The prayer of silence is a *faith* practice. It's not about knowledge. It's about recognizing our littleness and God's greatness, which is why the small child is such an appropriate image.

There is another Mary who is a great example of wordless faith—Mary, the mother of Jesus, who "treasured up all these things, pondering them in her heart" (Luke 2:19). I love the way Madeleine L'Engle, in her poem "After Annunciation," speaks about Mary's faith:

> This is the irrational season
> When love blooms bright and wild.
> Had Mary been filled with reason
> There'd have been no room for the child.[3]

Filled with reason, we privately wonder if we will get anything out of this silent prayer. Is God quietly waiting for us to stop talking and be still? Might he not be waiting for us to listen with our hearts? Is it possible that the soul of a weaned child is exactly what God is looking for in us? Is it possible that this is the only way he can make us whole?

Remember, Elijah's God spoke to him, not in the earthquake, the wind, or the fire but in "a gentle whisper" (1 Kings 19:12 NIV). In the deep silence we will find the Lord waiting for us. Wordless communication is an almost forgotten skill in our noisy, word-filled world. And we may find that coming to God in silence, without an agenda, is a welcome change as we drop the smoke screen of words that we use to protect ourselves.

Most of us would be awestruck and lost for words if we were presented to the president, the pope, any of the European or British royals, or even a sports legend like Michael Jordan. Is it so incongruous that in one portion of our daily prayer time we should be silent before the

Lord—not because we are scared but because it's a time to be with God without words?

Awed silence is an automatic response when you catch a glimpse of a full moon rising or see a spray of orchids growing in an unexpected place or watch a breathtaking aerial display by the U.S. Navy's Blue Angels or hear a superb voice hit just the right notes in a musical piece. Awed silence is a natural response to an expanded awareness of the loving mystery that is God.

Like a little child coming to a loving parent, we can expect an openhearted welcome when we turn our faces toward the Lord in silent prayer. As we take the step of faith and quiet our souls, we enter into the silence, into the cloud of unknowing, into the prayer of love. There, as we compose and quiet our souls, we will be like a weaned child—our souls will be like a weaned child within us.

14

Gazing on the Lord

Turn your eyes upon Jesus,
Look full in His wonderful face . . .

Helen H. Lemmel

Your child turns a somersault, makes a basket, hits a ball, runs a race, takes a dive, swims a few strokes, and with every one of these milestones, or new accomplishments, the cry is, "Look at me, Mommy!" "Watch me, Daddy!" How many times have you heard a child say that? Why do they say, "Look . . . watch . . ."?

Is there something special that happens when someone *looks* at us? Yes! Something special does happen. We are affirmed! When I look at you, my looking says that you are worth looking at, worth noticing, that you are worth my attention. It also says that I feel that I am worth something.

How often have you had a small child climb onto your lap, put his head close to yours, and actually take hold of your head and turn your face so that your eyes can focus nowhere else but on his eyes? Isn't this little child wise? There's an innate wisdom in children that tells them that love is communicated by looking, by turning their eyes onto the object of their love.

When I can't look at someone, there is something seriously wrong in my heart. Often it is filled with unforgiveness or guilt. Either one will damage me. A person with a poor self-image will frequently keep his eyes downcast in the presence of others. The person is ashamed in one way or another; he is afraid of not being accepted. Often he expects disapproval, knowing, instinctively, that it will be evident in someone else's eyes. Paradoxically, if the person would just look, he might see love and acceptance instead.

Almost universally people look into the eyes of people they like. Don't you look long into your loved one's eyes? When you first fell in love, you spent hours looking at each other, because that's what lovers do. They can never get enough of looking at the beloved. If we love someone, we will look into his or her eyes as much as possible. It is often through that same looking directly into another's eyes that people who have never met recognize a mutual attraction, even before any words have been exchanged.

My dad had five brothers, and so I had five wonderful uncles. Every one of them loved nothing better than to scoop up a little niece or nephew into a big bear hug and, putting forehead to forehead, look deep into that little one's eyes. To their dying days, each of these uncles remained the same, though the bear hugs ceased when they became too frail. Then it was simply hands on shoulders, head to head, eyeball to eyeball contact, and a deep, loving voice saying, "Hello, darling. Gee, it's good to see you!"

As a small child, I was puzzled by the words of one uncle, who always said, "You are a sight for sore eyes!"

"Do you have sore eyes, Uncle Russ?" would be my concerned reply.

"Not now, darling. Not now," was his response.

Perhaps God would say the same thing when he looks at us! His eyes "move to and fro throughout the earth" (2 Chron. 16:9), looking out for us, just like a parent waiting for a child to come home from an outing. His gaze is on us, whether we are aware of it or not. He waits for us to lift our heads, turn our eyes upon him, look full in his wonderful face, and return his look of love! We receive his gaze, we receive his love, and he receives ours.

Unless we are free of shame, we cannot look anyone full in the face. We find it hard to receive love and to give love. God offers us freedom from shame when he offers us his forgiveness, love, and acceptance. Our guilt, our anxieties, and even our crushing schedules fade into the background and become strangely dim as we step out in faith and gaze into the face of Jesus.

Remember the words of this hymn?

> Turn your eyes upon Jesus,
> Look full in His wonderful face;
> And the things of earth will grow strangely dim
> In the light of His glory and grace.[1]

In the light of God's glory and grace, the cares of this world take a backseat—if we will let them. When we become *quiet in his presence* and give ourselves to God, we turn our backs on everything else and, with single-eyed focus, face him. Because in silent prayer we give up our own thoughts, demands, and agenda, it is more God-focused and less me-focused than other forms of prayer.

From birth, we learn about how special we are when people show us love—especially through being looked at with love—and when they tell us they love us. Watch a mother with her new babe. She glows as she looks adoringly into the eyes of her precious little one. The baby stares back, struggling to focus on the mother. The special look and touch of love wordlessly combine to affirm to the baby that he is accepted, approved of, and loved. When a new babe comes into our home, we spend long hours gazing at this wondrous new life, thereby assuring the child of his welcome into our world.

Babies listen for the sounds of love, even though they don't know what is being said. Parents talk to them, sing to them, "bill and coo," and make all sorts of crazy "baby sounds" to reassure them that this new world into which they have been thrust is a safe place. Words they don't understand are spoken to them; songs they don't understand are sung to them; books they don't understand are read to them; toys they don't understand are given to them. For some babies, promises they don't understand are made on their behalf at their baptism. They are looked at, held, stroked, and cared for; and their world is filled with affirmations of how very special, loved, and precious they are.

Even when they make a mistake or have a little accident, they are quickly reassured by a loving look, and it is taken care of, accepted, excused, and forgotten. Loving caretakers focus on what precious little persons babies are—not on their behavior—and these little ones respond to unconditional love by returning love and adoration in large measure.

As children grow out of babyhood, however, their caretakers' attitude toward them changes. The ideal state of total acceptance, approval, love, and affirmation ends. Their mistakes and accidents are no longer met with looks of love and a lighthearted "Oops!" Now, the look they get is often a scowl of annoyance. This is one of the ways in which they receive the deep wounds that finally make them afraid to look full in the face of another person.

Why does the ideal state of total acceptance, approval, love, and affirmation have to end? Certainly, as children grow, they have to learn that some behavior is not acceptable to society and that some behavior has negative consequences. But how drastic does the change in the way adults relate to children have to be? As children grow older, why does the show-and-tell love virtually cease, to be replaced by a *stingy* expression of approval, love, and affection?

It's the feelings that parents have about themselves that get in the way of lavishing extravagant love on the precious charges God has given them. Most of us have wounds from our childhood, and we are still plagued by shame and guilt. Because of it, unless we have been overwhelmed by God's grace and become tenderhearted, we would rather tell others of their shortcomings than show them that they are loved. We can't change this behavior until we personally experience God's unconditional forgiveness.

Sitting humbly under the gaze of our loving God day after day in contemplative prayer, we will find that a change takes place in our perception of ourselves and of others. As we sit in silence in his loving presence, gazing in adoration at the Lord, we will find ourselves becoming like the One we adore! We will gradually be transformed, and even if the healing of our wounded psyche was not uppermost in our mind when we turned to God, the healing we need will begin.

St. John of the Cross speaks of the power of his beloved Lord's gaze: "When you were looking on me Your grace was printed in me by Your eyes."[2]

As our perception of ourselves changes, so will the way we look at our world. We will find ourselves becoming tender toward others. We will even begin to see things from their perspective, instead of always from our self-centered viewpoint. The pain, injustice, and tragedies that are all around us will begin to break our heart!

I live on the outskirts of Chicago. Around the world the name of this great city generally evokes images of mob violence, gangster shoot-outs, corruption, and '60s race riots. Far away from areas that are currently plagued by drive-by shootings, drug and gang wars, grinding poverty, crime, and frequent home and apartment fires that daily threaten the lives of their inhabitants, my suburban neighborhood is quiet and safe. It's sad that some of the white residents do not wish to see people of color in their midst—except, of course, for the teams of Hispanics who come during the day to do landscaping and housecleaning. Village officials, police officers, and ordinary citizens all maintain a vigilant watch for potentially troublesome strangers, taking particular note of people of color.

Years ago a black woman friend who lived nearby told me of her anxiety for her unborn son. She said, "I'm really afraid to bring a black son into this world. I'm afraid for his life. I know it will be hard for him to survive to adulthood and that life will be harder for him than for my daughter."

I was really surprised by her concern, but it made me think about the consequences of looking at people according to their outward appearance, instead of looking at them through the eyes of our Creator, who looks at the heart. Every time we look at someone, we can choose to gaze on him or her with contempt or with compassion. We can see people through the eyes of fear or the eyes of love. We can see ourselves as the protectors of our quiet, safe, color-free enclaves, or we can reach out and get to know those who are different and let them enrich us.

131

Since we are God's forgiven people, let's choose to be God's peacemakers, looking at all people with love and welcoming them into our midst. If we choose to see people differently, perhaps our neighbors will follow in our footsteps as we embrace all the races that live in our land, instead of building barriers of fear to keep us apart. Looking people full in the face, right into their eyes, we can give them the approval that God has given to us. Let's take the time to do it. With a look, we can speak wordlessly to them from our loving heart, letting them know that they are loved and accepted. We no longer have to be stingy. We can give as God gives, out of an abundant heart of love.

Our loved ones, our coworkers, our fellow worshipers, and our neighbors will all blossom if we make show-and-tell love a natural part of who we are. We can pass on to others what we have learned is true of us— that we are wonderful, special, precious, and unique. Not one of us is so busy, so important, that we can't pause for a moment and acknowledge the wonder of that other human presence and affirm him or her by a look of love.

We all carry within us our own personal image of God. When we come to him in prayer, it is to that image that we come. As we open ourselves to him in the prayer of silence and personally experience his forgiveness, acceptance, and healing, our distorted image of God will begin to change.

For some of us, a look turned to God is as effective to ward off distractions in our centering prayer times as is a love word. By directing our gaze toward the One who we know is gazing on us with love, we can quickly return to our intention.

Dare you put this book down at this very moment and practice gazing on the Lord? For a moment give him your complete attention—your whole self!

One of my favorite worship songs is "Gaze upon the Lord." A Poor Clare nun, in Dublin, Ireland, took the words of a love poem to the Lord written in the twelfth century by Clare of Assisi—the founder of the Poor Clares—and put it to music. The words and music are such a wonderful meditation to lead into contemplative prayer—and to keep me focused while there—that I personally use the song that way.[3] Here are a few of the words:

> Gaze upon the Lord,
> Gaze upon His face;
> Gaze upon the One
> who holds you in His embrace.[4]

These words tell us to gaze on the Lord in whose loving embrace we are always held. It is calling on us to behold the One who loves us and who, like the mother of a newborn, can't keep his eyes off us! He longs for us to turn our eyes on him, to return his look of love. When we do, we say yes to all that God has given us, to all that we are, and also to our unconditional surrender of our ego-centered life.

Really looking at someone, giving that person my complete attention, is the very least I can do if I love the One whom I claim to love—the Creator of all of us. Every human being is a one-of-a-kind, never-to-be-repeated miracle from God. Each person in our lives—whether a close family member or the person working the checkout at the grocery store—deserves to be treated with profound respect.

When we turn our eyes on Jesus in the prayer of silence, we find his gaze is already on us. The loving, compassionate gaze of God is saying to us: *You are my beloved, and I delight in you.*

As we give ourselves up to his tender gaze, we are assured of his love for us, and we will not be able to stop ourselves from responding: *You are my Beloved, and I delight in you, Lord!* When we are secure in our place in his heart, we are free to go out into the world, gazing on everyone we meet in the same gentle and compassionate way that he gazes on us.

Part 3

How Being Quiet in His Presence Changes Your Life

For busy people in a hurry to bring the whole world to Christ, spending an hour in silent adoration, without words, images, even with little affection—above all, with little concrete criterion that anything is happening, even that they are really praying—seems like a waste of time. This is perhaps the main reason why there are so few contemplatives in our Western world that is so geared to knowledge.

Contemplation is basically a look turned toward God. It is a human being standing, as it were, outside of the habitual ideas that he has of himself, the person that he thinks he is. It is his getting down below that false everyday ego and getting into his deepest source where he stands before God, consciously turning toward his Source, his Origin.

It does not consist in having beautiful thoughts, nor in having any emotions, sentiments, or piety. It consists fundamentally in standing before God, not with one faculty perceiving some facet of God but with one's total being absorbed into the total being of God. It is the return of my whole being back to God as a gift that expresses the attitude which I call worship-prayer, the ultimate point of contemplation.

But to reach this state of being in God—communicating with him, not in words or images, but in the silence of a yes continually spoken—requires a long process of dying to false self. And we are so reluctant to die!

George A. Maloney
Inscape and
The Breath of the Mystic

15

No Measuring Stick

But the LORD told Samuel, "Don't look at his appearance.
. . . God does not see as humans see. Humans look at
outward appearances, but the LORD *looks into the heart*."

1 Samuel 16:7 GOD'S WORD

In the days of Samuel, even those closest to God were
surprised when David was chosen to replace Saul. "The
Lord told Samuel, '. . . God does not see as humans see.
Humans look at outward appearances, but the Lord
looks into the heart'" (1 Sam. 16:7 GOD'S WORD). God
could see Saul's heart, and he could also see David's
heart. He wasn't nearly as interested in David's appearance or his performance as he was in his heart.

We worship the same God as David did, and when we
come to him, it is our *heart intention* that God looks at.
When our heart calls us to come to the Lord in silent
prayer—the prayer of love—we need to be aware that
though this is a simple practice, it is *not easy*. Despite
the best of intentions, our minds are full of distracting
thoughts about all the things we have to do, the places

we have to go, the phone calls we have to make, the groceries we have to buy. That's because we are "spirit beings having human experiences," as the saying goes. The Lord dwells in us and is one with us, but we are fragile, temporal creatures.

When we sit down with the intention of just *being* with the Lord for ten or twenty minutes, our busy thoughts do not obligingly stop. In fact, right from the beginning of our time with the Lord, it seems that those "vagrant thoughts"[1] crowd in insistently, "demanding to know what we are doing,"[2] as *The Cloud of Unknowing* puts it. It is at this time that we simply focus for a moment on our love word, saying it very slowly and gently to ourselves. Whenever we find ourselves being badgered again by a distracting thought, it's time to use our love word.

It is the intention of our heart that brings us to God, and, just as with King David, it is that intention that our loving God sees. He sees our desire to give ourselves to him. The Lord does not judge or condemn us for something we cannot do, any more than a loving parent judges and condemns a tiny baby for what he or she can't do.

When children are little, they want to be big. Each birthday for them is a time for celebration, as much for the fact that they are one year older as for the cake and presents. Growing up is important to children. Some families have a measuring stick on the wall for the children to periodically stand against to gauge their progress toward full stature.

Unfortunately, many of us carry a measuring stick in our heads. We use it to take the measure of others, and we use it constantly on ourselves. Even in our faith lives, we are notoriously vigilant about measuring ourselves. We have heard that faith is not about what we do, yet we can't help it. When ill fortune strikes, our first thought is: *What have I done to deserve this?* When we've done something good, we look around to see if it was noticed by anyone who can reward us! We certainly hope that God noticed!

When I think about my relationship with God, it's easy for me to forget that we are lovers and slip into the "How am I doing?" game. Bad habits die hard and, unless I catch myself, I find that I get out my measuring stick to see how I'm doing. In the most important part of my relationship—the times of intimacy with my Lord—when I dig out my mental report card, I am in trouble. This is when the black marks really show up. "Twenty minutes promised today, Lord, but it seems as if nineteen minutes were spent thinking about grocery shopping, washing the car, someone's birthday, and so on." In the early days of my practice, I used to get depressed at my poor performance and would decide, "I'm no good at this." I was often tempted to give up. I'm so glad that I didn't.

When we come to practice centering prayer, we can trust God to see the *intention* of our heart. Then we have to act on that trust and resist the temptation to reach for the measuring stick to see how we did or get out the report card to grade ourselves. Instead, as an act of faith, we simply say, "Thank you, my Love, that you see the desire of my heart and that you love me."

Michael Molinos, a seventeenth-century Spanish Jesuit who was persecuted as a heretic for teaching inward prayer, wrote in *The Spiritual Guide:* "When the time to be before the Lord has come, know that your friend *faith,* and your friend *intention,* will guide and conduct you to God."[3]

Contemplative prayer is above all a prayer of *faith.* Know that when you embark on this journey of prayer you are accompanied, as Michael Molinos said, by your friend *faith* and your friend *intention.* Remember that your Beloved has his eyes fixed on you with a look of love. We have to trust that God *sees* our intention to give ourselves to him and believe that he's not mad at us when we find ourselves carried away by an enticing thought. We have to turn our backs on the temptation to judge ourselves.

Judging ourselves as good or bad is foolishly taking from the Tree of the Knowledge of Good and Evil, the tree that caused Adam and Eve so much heartache. When we focus on the Tree of the Knowledge of Good and Evil, we live a narrow life of legalism—we live from a personal list of dos and don'ts. We forget about grace, about God's unconditional love for us, and wrongly assume that the Lord passes out brownie points when we do "good" and demerits when we do "evil." In Colossians, Paul minces no words about this false approach to life: "If you have died with Christ to the elementary principles of the world, why, as if you were living in the world, do you submit yourself to decrees, such as, 'Do not handle, do not taste, do not touch!'?" (Col. 2:20–21).

The Tree of Life, God's permanent, indwelling presence, is his gracious alternative to living by dos and don'ts. Most of us know the words in Galatians—"It is no longer I who live, but Christ lives in me" (2:20)—but we live our lives oblivious to the profound mystery of our union with our indwelling Lover. We have taken from the Tree of Life—the Lover of our souls, the Lord—and it is on him that we need to stay focused. Like Peter, when he climbed out of the boat and walked on the water toward the Lord, we are foolish if we take our eyes off Jesus to look at how we are doing. It's really none of our business. It's God's business.

God sees the intentions of our heart and he loves us unconditionally. There is truly nothing we can do to be any more loved by God than we already are. He created us for himself, and he loves each one of us for who we are. As we come to him in the prayer of silence day after day, his loving presence forces us to face whether we really believe this truth or not.

"Oh," you say, "I know that God loves me. I know that I can't earn my salvation or earn my way into God's good graces."

But do you? Do I? Do we as Christians really *know* that there is nothing we can do to be any more loved by God than we already are, that there are truly no "I love you, *but* . . ." conditions to God's love? Do we believe that "my Father is very fond of me"? Or is this just one of those things that we feel we have to say? We say it, but do we believe it is true for *us?*

My family gathered around the afternoon tea table, which was laden with freshly baked scones, cookies, cream-filled sponge kisses, and one of my mother's special treats, a devil's food chocolate cake. My dad winked at my mother as she set glasses of milk before my brother, my sister, and me and began to pour the tea for her and Dad.

"Whose cake is it?" my father asked us, pointing with the cake knife to the chocolate cake he was about to cut.

We three children all looked at each other. What was he up to?

"It's your cake," I ventured tentatively.

"Yes. It's my cake, isn't it, Mother?" Dad said, looking at her again. My mother smiled and nodded.

He took the large knife and began cutting the cake. Instead of cutting the pieces evenly, however, he cut some really thin pieces and some fatter ones.

My brother and sister and I all gave each other a puzzled look.

Again my dad asked, "Whose cake is it?"

"It's your cake!" we three said together, anxious for him to get on with it and pass out the cake.

He carefully lifted a piece of cake and placed it on a plate. When all of the five plates had cake on them, he pointed to the plates—some of which had a large piece and some a small piece—and asked again, his gray-green eyes twinkling, "Whose cake is it?"

Puzzled, we replied in a singsong chorus, "It's your cake, Daddy!"

"So, if it's my cake, I can do what I like with it, right? I can give it to you or I can give it to our neighbors or I can feed it to the chooks [chickens]?"

"Yes."

"So, if I give one of you a large piece and one of you a small piece, you will both have more cake than you have now, won't you?"

"Yes."

"It's my cake, and I can do what I like with it, can't I?"

I remember thinking at the time, *He's going to give it to the chooks! We're not getting any!*

Then, I looked at my mum, and she was still smiling. No. He wasn't going to throw her beautiful chocolate cake away.

My dad carefully took a plate and put it in front of my mum, then my sister, then my brother, then me, and finally he took one for himself. Our pieces were of various sizes.

"Eat your cake and enjoy it. *One* word about the size of the piece you have, or the size someone else has, and you will lose your piece. It's none of your business what I give to anyone else. Keep your eyes off what other people have. Let's eat!"

We all proceeded to eat and enjoy our cake. No one said a word about the size of the pieces. And then we all got second helpings. I no longer remember who got the most cake. I only remember that it was Dad's cake!

My father hated greed and waste, but even worse than that, he hated whining. He expected us to be thankful and appreciative. He wanted us to gratefully and gracefully accept the gifts that life handed us without measuring them against what someone else had. He knew that life isn't always fair and that if we had a quid pro quo or reward and punishment mentality, life would be very hard for us. He wanted us to know that he loved us unconditionally, regardless of the size of the piece of cake he gave us!

It is perfectly natural for us to think that our behavior determines how much we are loved. We make a mistake when we think that God's love for us is connected to our behavior when it's not. He loves us unconditionally. Regardless of how well we perform, he always has a warm welcome for us, his beloved.

Jesus came to show us God's love. He longs for us to accept that love, to come boldly into his presence, and to fling ourselves into his arms. God is the adoring, loving One who is watching and waiting for us to come to him.

The Song of Songs likens our relationship with God to that of bridegroom and bride. The picture is not that of an old married couple who are bored with each other. The picture here is poignant—they can't wait to be alone together. In our society, it is the tradition for the bridegroom to wait for the bride. Sound familiar? Isn't our Bridegroom playing the waiting game too? How long does he have to wait to have us fling ourselves into his arms? How long does he have to wait to be loved for himself, without being presented with a list of things we want, things for him to do, and things about which we are anxious?

King Saul of Israel was the cutest guy around. This is how he was described: "There was not a more handsome [person] than he among the sons of Israel. . . . he was [head and shoulders] taller than any of the people" (1 Sam. 9:2). But God replaced him with David, the youngest son of Jesse. Why? God spoke favorably about David. He said, "I have found David son of Jesse a man after my own heart" (Acts 13:22 NIV). Here, long before Christ came to earth, is a clue to what the Lord sees when he looks at us.

Can this possibly be true for us too, that the Lord is looking at our heart, seeing our intention to love and adore him? Does he see our faith and trust in him and, as he did with Abraham, does he reckon it to us as righteousness (see Gen. 15:6)?

The Scripture tells us that "a thousand years [is] as a day" with God (2 Peter 3:8 NOAB). Perhaps God would prefer a moment of our heart intention, rather than hours and hours of time spent in Bible study, long wordy prayers, and doing good works.

If the grace of God means anything, it means that God doesn't care as much about what we *do*, as he cares about *us*. He wants us to give ourselves to him, unreservedly, just as a little child gives himself to loved ones and just as a bride and bridegroom give themselves to each other.

Could it be that our Betrothed, our Beloved, has no yardstick by which he measures us, that there is no report card, that he requires no good deeds, not even a clean slate when we come to him? Could it be that he wants us to come to him as we are and come to him for *himself*? Could it be that all he wants of us is that we give ourselves to him as wholeheartedly as we possibly can and that we completely forget about how we are doing as we immerse ourselves in his loving presence? Perhaps this is the good news of Jesus Christ that we have seldom heard!

I believe the only way to break the habit, which is so ingrained in our culture, of checking to see if we measure up is to practice seeing from God's perspective. Contemplative prayer is an excellent way to practice that

144

new seeing. We soak ourselves in the words of truth: God looks at the heart intention not at our performance. He welcomes us as a beloved, precious, spotless bride. He calls us friend not servant. He sees us as an adorable, humble child. Then we come boldly into his presence to be held in his arms as we practice just being with him; and he begins the process of making us whole in the silence.

As we sit in his presence day after day, we will become more and more certain that we are loved, and we will be less likely to focus on our performance. Once we see how much he loves us, then our natural response is to love him, and others, in return. As we recognize ourselves as his beloved, we will gradually become love to others.

Let's just take the Lord at his word. Let's enjoy him for himself, and let's accept that we are truly his beloved! Let's throw away our report cards and our measuring sticks and learn to ignore that critical inner voice that never has anything good to say about us. Let's come boldly into the arms of our Lover, knowing that he *looks at the intention of our heart.*

145

16

Being the Beloved

Being in love is different from plain loving. I may love many people; but if I am in love . . . the thought of my loved one is always in my mind and heart like the small fire or the murmuring stream. [My lover] dwells in me and I in her.

William Johnston

As I drove, the oldies station on the car radio was playing a Neil Diamond song. As I listened to the words, I thought, "Sadly, this is the experience of all too many people, including me—no flowers, no love songs. In fact, as the song says, 'You hardly talk to me anymore.'"

I remembered when my husband-to-be and I, starry-eyed, had vowed to each other that the magic would never wear off. We'd be different; we'd always be lovers; we'd always treat each other as the beloved. We would never become disenchanted, embittered old married folks. I remembered how I had hoped and prayed that I would be able to keep my vows, as I buried my misgivings about this second marriage into which I was entering. But we did become disenchanted, embittered "old married folks"—so disenchanted that the flowers, the love songs, and the talking all stopped, and we divorced. Why? Basically because we didn't live for the other person; we didn't realize that the "to die for" love of Jesus for his bride was an example for our marriage. Also we stopped acting like lovers—almost as soon as we married. We didn't nurture our love. We didn't talk. Blame was laid. Apologies were made. Life went on, but we had learned nothing from the experience that would help us the next time the problem arose. We both assumed that apologizing and trying to forget were the right things to do, but, without talking about what had happened, we never discovered the changes we needed to make to nurture our love. Finally, after many years of this lack of honest communication, there were no meeting points left.

In our love relationship with God, we Christians make the same mistake; we assume that what we are doing is right, and the rest is up to him.

A friend tells a story from his early teens when he was very shy. One day, as he sat at the front of the school bus, the prettiest girl in his class, Mary Ellen—who was sitting in the back of the bus—sent him a message. It said, "Mary Ellen thinks you're cute!" He never did pluck up the courage to speak to Mary Ellen, but as he thought about her message, it began to change his self-image. *How about that! She thinks I'm cute!* Fragile and insecure as we are, one simple incident like this can make all the difference in the world as to how we see ourselves.

God sends us a similar message: He thinks we are "cute"! In fact he is in love with us. The thought of us is constantly in his heart. He calls on us to respond to him as his beloved. He continues to woo us, speaking to us in a gentle whisper, with words of love, encouragement, praise, and appreciation.

Irish Jesuit William Johnston speaks eloquently about what it is to be in love: ". . . if I am in love . . . the thought of my loved one is always in my mind and heart like the small fire or the murmuring stream. [My lover] dwells in me and I in her."[1]

Is this how we are with God? Is the thought of him always in our mind and in our heart like a small fire or a murmuring stream? Are we aware that God dwells within us and that we dwell in him? Do we see ourselves "hidden with Christ in God" (Col. 3:3), clasped to his heart as he sits at the right hand of the Father or, hands joined, dancing in the circle of love with the Trinity?

Because we are being the beloved, then we will see our life with and in God day by day in a totally new light. We will truly be filled with joy regardless of our circumstances. His life is the fire that empowers our every moment. St. John of the Cross says of his Beloved: "O living flame of love! how soothingly you wound my soul in its profoundest center."[2] That same living flame of love dwells in our center, filling us with his gentle light and tender love.

Hidden with Christ in God, we will recognize as gifts from the Lord the many things that happen to us each day, and love and praise will flow from our lips whatever our circumstances. We will find we cannot help smiling, as we are nudged by our Beloved to notice the love notes strewn along our pathway.

The Scriptures use marriage to explain to our finite human minds the mystical union that takes place when that "living flame"—the Holy Spirit—comes to dwell in our center. When we become aware of the life of the Spirit within us, many of us are filled with passion and zeal for God, and we want to go abroad as missionaries or into "full-time Christian work." That starry-eyed

148

euphoria we experience is akin to falling in love, and for some it truly is a falling in love with Jesus that is forever life changing.

Sadly, however, all too many Christians find that John's words to the church at Ephesus could have been written directly to them: "I know your deeds and your toil and perseverance. . . . But I have this against you, that you have left your first love" (Rev. 2:2, 4).

The people of Ephesus stopped being lovers. Being in love with God lost its appeal. Other things took their attention, the thought of him left their minds, and they left their first love. God was not the one at fault. His love didn't grow cold. He didn't give up on the Ephesians. And he doesn't give up on us. He continues to be enamored with us, always eager for us to turn our faces toward him.

When we ponder the love that God has for us, the lengths he has gone to capture our hearts, and the tender care that he shows us, we will find ourselves falling in love with him. After sitting trustingly and silently in his presence day after day, we realize one day that William Johnston's description of *being in love* has become true for us too. The thought of our beloved Lord is always in our heart, like a "murmuring stream." We are more and more aware of his indwelling presence and of his gentle whisper of love, speaking quietly to us in the depths of our being.

When we get caught up in our own selfish pursuits—caring more about what the world thinks of us than we care about our indwelling Lover—we tune out that whisper. Gradually our eternal Lover becomes dim and distant. We do our own selfish things, or we rush about doing unselfish works for the Lord. But it's all the same. We are neglecting our love relationship with the Lord; we are not being the beloved. A one-sided love relationship like this has no spark.

The Neil Diamond song on my car radio continued on about how natural it was to "talk about forever." But what happened to our "forevers" with God? As starry-eyed Christians, there are choices to be made if our love is to grow. We can choose to live in our self-centered way, drowning out the gentle whisper that tells us to turn wholeheartedly to God, or we can choose to give up our self-centered way to find great joy in the arms of the Beloved. If we see our relationship with God as a mutual admiration society, giving and receiving from an abundant heart of love, our love will grow, spilling over to others who will be blessed with the life flowing from it.

My parents, both now deceased, mirrored for me how wonderful a love relationship can be. They had a mutual admiration society. Each loved, appreciated, admired, and encouraged the other—privately, and in the presence of others. They were gentle and kind lovers who truly respected each other. There were never any snide remarks or sniping, nor was there ever tongue-in-cheek praise for the benefit of outsiders. When you were with them, you could feel their love for each other; it radiated out from them, embracing everyone in their world.

My school friends loved to spend a weekend at my house, because they were included in and embraced by the love that permeated our home. My parents were not blind to each other's faults, but neither did they use "subtle" hints to bring about change. They totally accepted each other.

My parents met and married in their thirties. My dad was the stay-at-home middle child in a family of eight surviving children. His five brothers and two sisters were very active in sports and social events in the Australian country district in which they lived. Their large farm was a long way from the nearest town, so they had their own football field, cricket pitch, plus a couple of tennis

150

courts. They had formed their own teams with their nearest neighbors, and my dad often played when the matches were at home. Unlike his siblings, he had never dated.

My mother was gregarious, adventurous, energetic. She loved sports, especially tennis, which she was really good at, and she loved to dance. Engaged to be married twice in her twenties, she had broken both engagements, unable to marry someone she didn't really love. Still single in her thirties, she didn't expect to meet anyone else who would want to marry her. Her home was quite a distance away from my dad's, but they lived in the same sports district. One of my father's younger brothers brought her home to the farm one weekend for a tennis tournament in which they were both playing. My shy dad and my "old maid" mum met during that tennis tournament and quickly fell in love. Soon afterward, they were married.

My dad loved and adored my mother. He would hold her hand and sing love songs to her. He considered himself the luckiest man in the world, and he felt that their meeting was a miracle. For someone like my mother to love him, the *least* of all the brothers, was always a miracle to him, a great gift to him from a loving God. My father promised her that he would always love her and do whatever he could to make her happy—and he did. He loved to surprise her with unexpected gifts. In a casual conversation, she might have mentioned to someone something she wanted or admired. Dad, who always had his ears tuned to her every word, would have heard and before long would present the gift-wrapped item to her.

As children, when we sat at the dinner table, we got used to my mother saying, "Would you serve the dessert, please? Daddy has hold of my hand and won't let me get up." Even after their fiftieth wedding anniversary, any time they walked together or sat at the table or on the couch, they held hands. Taking her hand, my dad would look into my mother's eyes and say, "You're a wonder!" (Mum would always give an embarrassed giggle and say, "Oh, Bill!")

God sees us as wonders. He loves us and sings love songs to us. We are miracles. We are gifts to him. God—the ultimate Lover, who laid down his life for his spouse—continues to pour himself into his relationship with us, his beloved. Even though we are in union with him, he continues to court us, just as any wise spouse will.

Years ago a gentle young man of my acquaintance made this statement after a promising courtship broke up: "I've decided that I'll wait to marry until I meet someone who is as prepared to die for me as I am to die for her."

He did meet that person, and they did marry. She was worth waiting for!

Our Lord speaks to me with the gentle, loving promptings of his Spirit within. He sings me love songs, and he longs for me to listen. He wants me to be as aware of his presence as he is of mine. He is waiting for the time when I am conscious moment by moment of his living in my heart. Even when I am not paying any attention at all to him, he is tuned in to me, looking for ways in which he can bless me. He loves to shower me with blessings, even when I'm undeserving of them. When I momentarily forget him and follow my feelings into sin, he is ever faithful to forgive me and quickly restores me to my exalted place as his precious, pure bride, never again reminding me of my "slip."

God is calling us, his beloved, into his presence. He wants us to come apart and be alone with him. In the silence of the prayer of unknowing, when we have set everything aside for his sake, our indwelling Lover reveals to us how much he loves and cherishes us. As we bask in his loving embrace, we become aware that we are *being the beloved,* and we love and cherish him in return.

17

Letting Go

Our hearts . . . will not rest till they rest in you.

St. Augustine

My dad died in 1996, at age eighty-eight, after suffering for a number of years with Alzheimer's disease. During his final years, my relationship with him had to change dramatically—reversing our roles of parent and child. It's a perfectly natural change of roles as parents live into frail old age—but it's difficult letting go of the way things have always been.

My dad was in his seventies when he suddenly wanted to talk to us, his children, about what had been a forbidden subject when we were growing up—his World War II experience. It seems to me, looking back now, that talking was a necessary letting go for him of some troubling memories.

He had served in the RAAF (the Royal Australian Air Force) in New Guinea and adjacent islands during 1941 to 1943, a time when both Allied and Japanese forces were vying for control of those areas. He was, for many

153

lonely months, a sniper—first with the Australian forces and then with the Americans. He worked alone at night, pitting his wits and skill against stealthy enemy invasion. Having grown up in the bush, he was self-reliant, was able to work alone, had an uncanny sense of direction, and was a crack shot (his family couldn't afford to waste ammunition—each shot meant fresh meat for a family of twelve).

Officially his job was as a night watch. None of his mates knew what he did or where he went. For all they knew, his kit-bag carried his lunch and perhaps a pencil and some paper to write a letter to my mother during the long night hours. Before he went out each evening, the commanding officer and he played cards in my dad's tent. Then they would pore over a map with the latest information on where the enemy was and plot where Dad was to go that night. Only he and the CO knew.

My father would pack his kit-bag—with his lunch, a flashlight, a hunting knife, a broken-down gun, and ammunition—and quietly leave the camp. Once he got to his secret place, he assembled the gun, put the knife in his belt, and waited.

As he spoke to us, he didn't give us any details. Looking way off in the distance, all he said, almost inaudibly, was: "It was them or us, darling." Pause. "I was good at my job." Pause. "It went on for a long time." Pause.

"Then one day the CO brought an officer from the U.S. forces to see me. The officer asked me if I would be willing to go north with him to do the same job for them. He said, 'We'll give you a commission. You'll serve as a member of the American forces. And we'll pay you in addition to your RAAF salary.' I thought about it for a few minutes, and then I said, 'I'll do this for you on one condition.' The officer said, 'Okay.' Then I said, 'I'll do this for you on the condition that I serve as an Australian and that I not be paid any differently from what my mates are being paid. That's what I want.' He accepted my condition. A couple of days later I went with him to the north."

For my dad, who treated everyone with great respect, the assignment he had during the war must have been incredibly hard. As he told us about it, he said, "I would never have done it, except I wanted a safe world for my children to grow up in."

During the confusing middle stage of Alzheimer's, he was frequently back in the tropics, running for his life through those jungles. A couple of times he even slipped out of the aged-care hostel, rapidly scaling the six-foot solid wooden fence surrounding the building before any of the much younger staff could stop him. Sometimes he was in a happier time, when he and his nine siblings were working on the farm or playing cricket or tennis.

When I visited him, on my short yearly sojourn in Australia, sometimes I would be his mother or his sister or my mother. By my Christmas 1994 visit, as the disease progressed, I had to acknowledge that my dad was gone, just as surely as was my mother, who had died earlier that year. My mother's death from smoke inhalation in the hostel fire was so painful for me that, especially to begin with, my broken heart could find solace and rest only when I sat in silence in the Lord's arms. In his loving presence, I found soothing balm for my battered soul.

As St. Augustine said, "Our hearts are made for you, Lord, and they will not rest till they rest in you."[1] During my visits with my dad, I had to let that rest completely engulf me. My family and I had to let go of the wise, mannerly, dignified father we had always known. He had been replaced by a helpless, often-querulous person, who, nevertheless, had the right to be treated with utmost dignity.

Sometimes my dad forgot what food was for.

"What's that?"

"That's your dinner."

"What do I do with it?"

"You eat it."

"How do I do that?"

"You pick it up with your fork, like this, and you put it in your mouth, like this, and you chew it, like this, and then you swallow it. Yum, yum."

"Oh, okay."

Sometimes he remembered everything about food except what to do with it once it was chewed. He stored it in his cheeks like a chipmunk and had to be reminded to swallow it. Like a child who is being potty trained, sometimes he had to be reminded to go to the toilet.

Whenever we visited with him, we had to let go of the fact that this was our father, who had wisely sat his family around his antique rolltop desk, spread out all the farm's expenses and income for us to see, and had a "business meeting" so that we would understand our family finances and responsibilities. This was our father, who, as shire president (mayor) of the country town we lived in, had the foresight to urge the setting aside of bushland before Melbourne's encroaching suburbs swallowed it all up. This was our father, who had farmed judiciously, surviving years of plenty and years of drought when many around him went bankrupt.

We had to let go of the dad of the past and embrace the dad of the present—but it was a grievous loss. He still looked much the same, but now he was stooped and he shuffled as he walked. In addition to Alzheimer's, he had the beginning of Parkinson's disease. A conversation with him was usually like a broken record. Every few minutes he'd ask the same question or make the same statement, because he had already forgotten what he had said a minute ago.

With my mother dead, and having spent the previous fifty-plus years in a very loving relationship, he craved love. So he would often say, "I love you"; "Give me a kiss"; "Give me a cuddle," to anyone who seemed familiar. Sometimes he was very angry and would swear the air blue; sometimes he was maudlin and cried all the time. The only way I could endure this distressing situation was to hold his hand when he would permit it and remember how much he had loved me when I was a tiny, willful child. Often, during these times, I would enter into the hermitage or silent place I had created inside myself for a few moments of *unknowing* prayer.

People who have no experience with dementia are often frightened or repelled by people with it, and they are unable to recognize them as persons anymore. Often an Alzheimer sufferer's family lacks understanding of what has happened to him or her, and they assume that the loved one is deliberately being difficult. Out of hurt and frustration, they are impatient and scold the helpless victim. My family and I knew that my dad was not responsible for his erratic behavior. Occasionally he would be back in the present with us and then, because he was aware of embarrassing us on a previous visit, he would apologize.

Even in his most difficult or depressed times, the one fact that reached into my dad's confusing world was that we loved him. All I had to do was touch his shoulders, look deep into his eyes, and say, "I love you, darling. I love you." The familiar words penetrated the swirling mists of confusion, he realized that he was safe, and often he would respond by leaning his head on my shoulder. Spirit touched spirit, the truth reached into his soul, and his body relaxed.

During my dad's last months, I found that I could not live in the past—even in the very recent past of a few minutes ago. Nor could I take anything he said or did personally. I had to let go of it all and just give myself completely to him in the fleeting *now*. Just as a mother does with a newborn, I had to live in the present moment. It was hard, but as I relaxed my grip on my life and made myself available to my dad in this final difficult phase of his life, I was to find peace and catch a glimpse of eternity.

Years ago, when I lived in Western Australia, I sat reading in my sunny terraced garden one afternoon. Nearby, stretching in about a four-foot circle, was a shimmering spider's web. In the middle of the web sat an enormous spider, perfectly still. Every so often a hapless insect bumbled into the web. With long, careful steps the spider slipped across the network of sticky silk and administered her anesthetizing jab. As the victim gradually became still, the good housekeeper wrapped her prize in a package of silk and then quickly returned to her watching post to await another candidate for her larder.

I watched, fascinated, as a pollen-laden honeybee hit the very perimeter of the web. In contrast to the other insects I had seen, as soon as the bee hit, she went completely still, immediately stopping her fragile wings before they became hopelessly entangled. As her legs were still free, she quickly rubbed the load of thick pollen from each one, tucked her wings into her sides, and, load-free and light now, she dropped to the ground, just as the spider reached her. She rapidly cleaned her wings, buzzed them a couple of times, and flew away. I thought of how many hours of work she had just jettisoned to be light enough to escape the deadly trap.

Whenever I seriously think of the false-self system that permeates our world and ourselves, I'm reminded of that bee. She was instantly aware of the danger she was in and of what she needed to do to survive. She needed to get rid of her bounty *fast.* In a brief moment the spider would reach her and it would be too late.

We too need to lighten our loads so that we can drop out of our entanglements. We know *so much*—about God, about psychology, about good and evil—but we find it so hard to let go. We *know* too much to come to God empty-handed, childlike. In all of life, and even in prayer, we set our agendas. Whether it's praise, piety, petitions, or penance, and whether it's good or evil, it's all added stuff that gets between God and us. We are so busy; our souls are so restless.

When we first came to God, we came empty-handed, accepting everything he had to offer us by grace. Now God is calling on us to jettison the loads we carry, just as the bee did, and come to him empty-handed again—humble and repentant. He wants to renew our minds, transform us, and show us how to love him and our world. We need to come to him with upturned hands. God's love expressed through us toward him and toward others *is* possible, but it's not our love—conditional; it's God's love—unconditional, with no nasty side effects and no strings attached.

To be healed of all the pain caused by conditional love, we have to set aside all agendas and seek God for himself. The prayer of the heart—waiting in stillness and in silence—is truly the only way we can let go of our focus on ourselves and put it on God. It's the only way to find our heart's desire, the *rest* in his loving presence that he promises.

Right at the end of his earthly life, Jesus gave us a graphic picture of what he desired in a follower. When Peter questioned him about the fate of one of the other disciples, Jesus replied, "What is that to you? You follow Me!" (John 21:22). In other words, "Love me with all your heart, Peter. And let go of everything else! That's all that's important! Let go so your heart can *rest in me!*"

Jesus speaks in the same way to us today: "Love me with all your heart! Let go of everything else! Your relationship with me is what's important. Let go so your heart can rest in me!"

Our loving God knows what is best for us, which is why he gave us the great commandment and the second one that is like it: to love God with every fiber of our being and to love others as ourselves (see Matt. 22:37–39). In a world that doesn't know how to love, we are called to let go of all that gets in the way of our loving God as he wants to be loved.

Let's come to him for himself, sit in silence in his presence, and allow his love to fill us. In him our hearts can truly find an oasis of peace and rest in the midst of our busy lives.

18

The Cloud of Forgetting

The labor, of course, is in the unrelenting struggle to
banish the countless distracting thoughts that plague
our minds and to restrain them beneath that *cloud of
forgetting.*

The Cloud of Unknowing

People who struggle with major wounds created by childhood abuse, whether verbal or physical, often experience
great difficulty in accepting help and in accepting themselves. They fear being vulnerable and trusting, especially
when they perceive that their vulnerability left them open
to the abuse in the first place. They find it hard to believe
that the adult abuser—and not the child victim—was the
one with the problem. We who have been abused have
to accept that we are not solely responsible for our
wounded psyche.

Becoming a whole person means accepting that my
wounds are not punishment meted out because I was
bad or unworthy. Believing this takes a giant leap of
faith, as well as a revelation of grace. Yes, both faith and

grace are God's business, but stepping into the circle of God's arms—into the safety of the cleft of the Rock, under the overshadowing wings—and being hid with Christ in God are the parts we play in becoming whole (see Col. 3:3).

When the Scripture says, "You must be perfect—just as your Father in heaven is perfect" (Matt. 5:48 GNB), the Greek word translated *perfect* means much more than that. It's related to the Hebrew word *shalom*, which means inner and outer peace, complete and total peace—or in a word, *wholeness*.

We begin our journey toward wholeness by taking a leap of faith and coming to God in silence—to bask in his presence, to be bathed in his love—to allow him to do his healing work. The author of *The Cloud of Unknowing* says, "the *labor*, of course, is in the unrelenting struggle" with our "countless" thoughts and in restraining them "beneath that *cloud of forgetting*."[1]

And it is hard work, indeed, this task to which we set ourselves, when we come to the prayer of silence, immerse ourselves in the cloud of unknowing, and struggle to cover everything with a cloud of forgetting. We have to forget everything, even the goodness and beauty of God's creation. If we are to lay aside all thoughts of our world—turning within, to the cloud of unknowing where the Lord dwells—then we must bury those thoughts in the cloud of forgetting.

When we go beyond thoughts, words, and emotions and open our hearts, our whole being, to God, we give ourselves to him as a gift. Immersing ourselves in the silence of contemplative prayer, we are placing our wounded selves in the hands of the loving Healer, who can make us whole.

My mother, being from sturdy Scottish stock, followed her family breakfast tradition by always cooking porridge for us all. Sometimes, if she was called away suddenly to help my dad with an animal or to help one of the children get ready for school, the porridge pot would be left sitting half on the hob and half on the edge of the woodstove to keep the porridge warm. If it sat there too long, the porridge would dry out and begin to stick. Sometimes it was forgotten and would begin to burn. When my mum finally remembered it, she would immerse the pot in water and leave it soaking in the sink.

When we take our leap of faith into our loving Healer, it's just as if God immerses us in clean, refreshing water. It's just like soaking that saucepan in which the oatmeal has burned. When the process first begins, nothing much moves, but, after a little while in the water, some of the oatmeal starts to loosen and float to the top. And then as the soaking goes on, gradually the older, deeper stuff starts to loosen and it too floats to the surface and drifts away. Eventually, all the burned porridge is loosened, it comes off, and the saucepan is sparkling clean again. In the same way, to have our deep psychic wounds healed, we have to stay immersed in God and allow all the built-up stuff to float away.

Some time ago my heart was touched when I received a letter from a seventy-year-old grandmother who was still suffering from the pain of childhood abuse. "You would have thought I'd have resolved all this by now," she wrote. "I feel guilty and selfish even acknowledging that fact and keep putting it away or pushing it down— and trying to get on with my life on a level I can cope with. But deep down I know all is not right and that I am not a whole person."

The fact that one's wounded state is being faced and acknowledged at all is what is important—not how long it has taken to do so. Facing the truth is always the beginning of healing; the next step is to accept our forgiveness, our feelings of guilt about the past, and our own inability to forgive; and then we must become as apparently self-centered as we need to be while admitting and working through the pain.

One evening recently I drove to a meeting with an elder of my church. It was dark in the parking lot when we met, and I was appalled to find myself in the grips of a horrifying flashback. Many, many years ago, I had been shocked on two occasions to find myself the victim of uninvited sexual advances by one of the pastors in my church. The first time it happened was in a darkened church parking lot as we were discussing the music for the next week's service. I scampered into my car, said a hasty "good night," and drove home. As I thought it over, I began to conclude that I had imagined it—or that it had been accidental. The pastor was a highly respected married man, an upstanding member of the community, a sought-after lecturer, as well as having a huge personal "fan club" in the church. *I must be mistaken.* I put it out of my mind and went on with my life.

After the Sunday evening service a couple of weeks later, when the same pastor declared that he had had his wife drop him off and needed a ride, I blithely offered to drive him home. Only after we got into the car and I drove out of the parking lot did I remember the previous incident. I was brought back to reality with a gut-wrenching thump when I found his hand on my thigh! I took his hand, put it onto the armrest between us, and continued driving. Fortunately he lived only a few minutes away. I screeched the car up to his door and couldn't wait for him to get out!

Now I knew it was no mistake—no accident! What was I to do?

My first instinct was to forget it and to make sure I was *never* alone with him again. But then I realized how much this would affect what was an essential part of my life. I weighed going to the other pastors of my church. Was it such a big deal? I hadn't been raped! It was just

164

my word against his. Why would they believe me—the word of a "nobody" woman member of the congregation against the word of a *pastor!* No. I had no hope. I thought that probably the best thing to do was leave the church. Then I began to think about this pastor. He was always surrounded by young people, especially pretty young women. *Hmmm.* How could I be sure that I was the only one it had happened to? What about those lecture tours he did? *Hmmm.* Did I have the right to hide, run away, protect my reputation, and risk potential damage to another young woman? One of my friends had been subjected to sexual abuse throughout her childhood, and it had taken her years of therapy to even begin to heal from it.

I concluded that I had to do something, so I made an appointment with the senior pastor, telling him that I had a very serious matter to discuss with him. As soon as I hung up the phone, I had second thoughts. Even though I had always trusted this pastor implicitly, I wondered if perhaps I was a naive fool.

To my utter amazement, when I told him of the two incidents, he simply nodded his head. He didn't seem to be surprised. He agreed that the best way to handle it was to invite the offending pastor to meet with both of us, and my job would be to confront him—to tell the story again, in exactly the same way.

Now, this was really scary! But that is what we did. I was speechless when the perpetrator hung his head and acknowledged that everything I said was true and that he wanted my forgiveness! He agreed to begin therapy. After a few months, to my great relief, he left our church and went to live a long, long way away.

The part about the whole experience that surprised me was how much damage these two tiny, insignificant incidents did to my psyche. For many months—maybe years—I struggled with depression. I withdrew from

165

church activities. I became very cynical and untrusting of people in ministry.

Even though I did some work with a therapist, the healing that I needed didn't really begin to take place until I began contemplative prayer. I didn't know what I needed to become whole, nor did I know what was happening. Truly we don't know what damage was done to us in the past; and we don't know how to access healing, but God knows. He made us in his image. He will restore us. He will make us whole.

I found, as I sat in silence and entrusted myself to the mystery of *unknowing,* that the cloud of forgetting began to swallow up the fear and the pain. The wounds created by having my trust violated began to heal, as I was immersed in God's love and his healing presence surrounded me.

The author of *The Cloud* explains the two essential parts to contemplative prayer as being *the cloud of unknowing* above us, in which the Lord dwells, and *the cloud of forgetting* beneath us, in which we restrain everything that will distract us from God. He says:

> If you wish to . . . take up the contemplative work of love as I urge you to, there is something else you must do. Just as the cloud of unknowing lies *above you,* between you and your God, so you must fashion a cloud of forgetting *beneath you,* between you and every created thing.[2]

We must *choose* to forget everything of this world—even our thoughts and words of praise for the Lord. We create—fashion—a *cloud of forgetting* between us and everything else and immerse ourselves in the *cloud of unknowing* that is our God. Forgetting and forgiving we cannot do alone, but if we are willing to do our part, God will do his.

166

When we have a life-threatening illness or need major surgery, we do not feel guilty and selfish for needing lots of rest, recuperation, understanding, and care in order to heal. Most of us have serious, life-threatening wounds to our soul—some of which require "major surgery." Our job is to trust the surgeon—God—and cooperate with him in the healing process, just as we do when we are healing physically.

In addition to regular times of contemplative prayer, there are things we can do to help slow us down and facilitate healing. We should notice the beauty of the world around us and appreciate God's gift-filled creation. He made us body, soul, and spirit and intends for us to live fully in all of these. He made our senses to help us fully enjoy life. Remember these words: "God saw all that He had made, and behold, it was *very good*" (Gen. 1:31). We should not be afraid to let our wise God's healing touch through our senses help repair and heal our wounded souls.

Here are some caring-for-yourself things to do: As evening draws near, light candles or soft lamps and play some gentle music. Go for long, leisurely walks and really look at and notice the clouds, the color of the sky, the patterns made by the tree branches, the shape of the leaves and the flowers; as you walk, listen to the sounds of life around you—the crunch of dry leaves or twigs underfoot and the scurrying of small creatures in the grass—feel the warmth of the sun or a breeze on your skin; sniff the air and savor the smell; listen for the birdsong in the early morning, during the day, in the evening. Look, listen, feel, savor—dare to enjoy your senses, and allow that childlike enjoyment to seep into your battered psyche.

We need to allow ourselves to be bathed and immersed in the beauty all around us. Plant seeds or seedlings in the rich, moist earth, look at them every day, and take the time to watch them grow. Buy an indoor plant that is about to flower (an orchid is a wonderful gift to yourself), and marvel at the Creator's lavish extravagance as the miracle of exotic, exuberant life unfolds day after day, week after week. Prepare a gourmet salad or dessert, using colorful, fragrant fresh herbs and/or tropical fruit; serve it in a glass bowl; and eat it slowly, savoring every bite, noticing the aroma, the texture, and the taste. Buy scented bath oil or salts and, at least once a week, light a potpourri candle, take the phone off the hook, put some beautiful music on your stereo, and take a long, fragrant, luxurious bath. Pamper yourself. Exult in your senses.

Don't feel guilty about all this "indulgence." This is a healing process, a recovery process. Being aware of the need to be gentle with your body, soul, and spirit is wise. Healing takes time. Be as faithful as you can to the regular practice of silent prayer, restraining everything—including all painful memories—beneath the cloud of forgetting, as you immerse yourself in the cloud of unknowing.

A little holy rejoicing at how "fearfully and wonderfully" God has made our bodies is in order. A little gratefulness to God for a world filled with good things for us to enjoy is not misplaced. A little appreciation of the beauty of God's good creation—including ourselves—will gradually become our spontaneous response as healing takes place.

One of my favorite reminders of this comes from a little prayer by Macrina Wiederkehr, a Benedictine nun who lives in Arkansas. It says:

> O God,
> help me
> to believe
> the truth about myself,

168

no matter
how beautiful it is![3]

God has given us the gift of imagination, and it can be used in a wonderful way. We can begin to crowd out harmful memories by seeing ourselves as one of the chicks that Jesus mentioned when he said, "How often I have longed to gather your children together, as a hen gathers her chicks under her wings" (Luke 13:34 NIV). Or we can see ourselves as one of the little children who clambered onto Jesus' lap, unafraid (despite the disapproval of the disciples), or as the weaned child resting against his mother, or as the bride coming into the bridal chamber to be with the Bridegroom.

We can see ourselves as the lost sheep for whom the Good Shepherd left the other ninety-nine. Notice that he did not scold that lost sheep. He rejoiced! And he returned to the flock happy because the lamb that had been lost was found. His flock was whole—complete—again.

Or we can see ourselves as the coin lost by the householder. She swept her house, found the coin, and threw a party to rejoice that the coin had been found. Her collection was whole—complete—again.

When Jesus speaks of himself as the Good Shepherd, he says that he knows us and calls us by name. He knows us. He knows each one of us and we are precious to him. Our work, our task, during this time of forgetting and healing is to accept the truth about ourselves, *no matter how beautiful it is.* We are more likely to be able to do that when we choose to be silent, to turn within, to put ourselves in a place where we are open to hear God's "gentle whisper" speaking words of love and approval to us.

Embrace the infant you, the toddler you, the first-grader you. Look at your early photos and imagine your adoring Creator looking at you with a look of love. See and experience the warmth and healing in that gaze. As you are able, carry his gaze throughout your life up to the present time. Think of specific times and roles—teenager, young adult, married person, parent, sibling, grandparent, employee, retired person, on holidays, birthdays, and so on. Then trust God, your Healer, to gradually take the sting out of your wounds, as you let go of them, as you cover them with the cloud of forgetting.

Our wounds won't ever totally leave; just like physical scars, they remain. But they become less and less painful as we identify ourselves with the Healer and see ourselves as precious to him. And, then, freed from guilt and shame, our attitude and actions toward other hurting, vulnerable people become much more gentle and loving and affirming—because we know a little bit about how awful they feel. Our own scars allow us to identify with them.

With our children, grandchildren, nieces, and nephews—especially little ones—we are free to express praise, to tell them how special, talented, and wonderful they are—and mean it! Our enthusiasm can inspire them to believe in their intrinsic goodness, and once they do, it grows. As our world and our loved ones become whole, we too become aware of our own gifts and talents. Then, without pride, we will be able to say, "I'm special. I'm wonderful. I'm a good relative/friend. And—I am *love!*" (If that's difficult for you, wink at God as you say it—and, believe me, you'll see him wink back! He loves secrets like that!) Remember, the Scripture says, "We love, *because He first loved us*" (1 John 4:19).

We all need to say, "Lord, I do believe; help me in my unbelief!" (see Mark 9:24). None of us is whole. And none of us is immune to the effects of the fall. We are all in need of redemption and restoration—a process that takes a lifetime. This is the faith life. Because we are made in his image, our loving God longs for us to be whole, complete, perfect—and we can be, if we will come to him and allow his loving presence to transform and heal us.

As we restrain all, including our pain and our praise, under the cloud of forgetting and immerse ourselves in the loving, nurturing prayer of unknowing, we will become more aware of how lovingly and tenderly God looks at us. We will be able to accept that we are precious in his sight and that the truth about us is beautiful. We will become aware that burning deep within us is a small fire of love. As we become whole, that small fire will begin to grow, eventually bursting into flame so that we will become aflame with the fire of his love.

19

Aflame with Love

When the day of Pentecost had come, they were all
together in one place. . . . And there appeared to them
tongues as of fire . . . and they rested on each one of
them. And they were all filled with the Holy Spirit. . . .
Everyone kept feeling a sense of awe.

Acts 2:1, 3–4, 43

The natural response to falling passionately in love is to
want the same for everyone else. And this was what happened to the first Christians. They were aflame with the
love of Jesus. They couldn't wait to tell the good news
to everyone they met! Barriers between people were
coming down. A great crowd gathered. And God turned
the Jewish celebration of the Feast of First Fruits into
a fiery love fest by visibly coming to dwell in his bride.
The people saw what appeared to be tongues of fire; they
heard the sound of rushing wind; they experienced being
filled with the Holy Spirit. And they couldn't contain
themselves. They were amazed at what God was doing
and shared what they had seen, heard, and experienced.

Others were caught up in the excitement, and they too decided to give God a chance. And once again, as they saw the work of the Holy Spirit, they were all filled with awe!

We are so familiar with the story that we miss the drama, the radical nature of the events unfolding throughout the Gospels and on into the Acts of the Apostles. What was happening on the day of Pentecost that they were filled with awe?

These early Christians grasped that God had a passionate desire to share his life with them. They realized that the Jesus story was a dramatic love affair of epic proportions. This was no ho-hum religious transaction between a legalistic ruler and the peons who were supposed to be caretakers of his property. This was a Lover wooing his beloved! This was an all-out assault on human complacency. God wanted humanity's attention! He wanted us to know that he was no longer going to be satisfied with dwelling in an ark, in a tent, or in a cold inanimate temple. Like any lover, he wanted to dwell in the heart of his beloved. We were made in his image. We were made for him. And he was coming to claim his own.

At the beginning of Jesus' ministry, the disciples had said to him, "Where do you live?" And his reply was, "Come and see" (John 1:38–39 GNB). He took them home with him. And then, for the next three years, they were with him. They learned about where he lived. He lived in the heart of the Father. And the Father lived in him.

At Pentecost it was time for God to take up residence in his bride. And that's what happened. God came as *fire* to dwell in his people!

As respectable, proper twenty-first-century people, we have relegated our passionate, resident God to a small compartment in our lives. We call on him only when we need a miracle, when we need comfort, or when we feel bad about something we have done.

We usually don't let him come out when we have guests in our home. And we don't let him get too involved in our good, busy lives. We do our grocery shopping, we cook our meals, we keep our houses clean and neat, and, as long as God stays in his place—in the closet—we will slip in and spend a minute with him once in a while. We even go to church and expect him to be there, but we don't want him to do anything that might embarrass us! In other words, we have been treating God like a pet spouse whose presence in our lives is decided at our whim.

Our God is a passionate God. He loves us to the point of dying for us, and he wants more than a peripheral role in the life of his bride. He is waiting, quietly and patiently, for her to take time out of all her busyness— making phone calls, organizing the kids, putting away the groceries—and come to him. He wants an intimate love relationship with each one of us. He wants to be in the center of our lives.

All we have to do is stop all the activity for a little while and turn our attention to the One who loves us, who dwells in the very center of our being. He has taken up residence in our hearts, and he is calling us to come home and *be* with him.

I had lived in an awareness of my union with Christ since the mid-'70s, but I hadn't really known what to do with that awareness, and I had been unable to find anyone who could tell me. In the early '90s my life was changing radically. I had begun, in 1986, to seek, through prayer and among the traditions of the church, a greater depth in my devotional life.

I knew that my spirit was one with the Spirit of Christ; I knew that I was Christ to my world and that I had the mind of Christ. I knew that God loved, accepted, and forgave me. I knew that my desire was his desire. But I wasn't satisfied with just knowing these things.

What I really wanted was what the saints from the past wrote of—a passionate intimacy with the Lord. I wanted to walk in the Spirit, manifesting those elusive fruits of love, joy, peace, patience, longsuffering, meekness, and self-control as a normal part of my life, instead of just occasional flashes on a good day.

Gradually, as I listened to God's voice through Scripture, books, other Christians, several retreat experiences, and through many quiet, thoughtful times with the Lord, I began to see that he was more than willing to show me the way into his heart. All I had to do was turn the radio and TV off, stop reading and thinking about him, set aside all that I knew about him, and make an intentional space in my day to be still and silent. I didn't know it to begin with, but he was calling me into contemplative prayer—the prayer of love.

For the risen Christ to become a reality to me, and for me to relate to God as an intimate friend, all that I knew about God needed to be set aside. All the busyness, all the activity, all the noise were very effectively blocking out the stillness and silence that were necessary for me to *listen* to God and for his living presence to become a reality to me. It all had to go.

I can't say it any better than it is said in *The Cloud of Unknowing:*

> . . . imagination and reason have taught you all they can and now you must learn to be wholly given to the simple awareness of your self and God . . .[1]

> A person who has long pondered these things [our own sinfulness, the Passion of Christ, and the kindness and goodness and dignity of God] must eventually leave them

175

behind beneath *a cloud of forgetting,* if he hopes to pierce the *cloud of unknowing* that lies between him and his God.[2]

After years of Bible study, growing in the knowledge of God, and pondering my own inadequacies and God's suffering, it seemed that I was being called to set it all aside to focus on God for himself. In other words, all I knew, good and bad, needed to be *forgotten* when I turned to God. I had to turn my back on everything I knew and, in faith, immerse myself in the ineffable God. Slowly I learned to be quiet. Sometimes I read a short passage of Scripture, allowing God to speak to me through it. But more often, I would become totally quiet, sitting in silence with the Lord without even words of praise. I discovered that centering prayer became more and more central to my prayer life, and through those times of centering prayer my desire for an experience of God and his love was fulfilled.

Occasionally now God seems so close that I don't need to seek him—but most of the time when I come home to be with him in the silence, I wait for him in faith. How do I wait? Micah gives me a clue. He asks a question and then gives the answer: "What does the Lord require of you but to do justice, to love kindness, and to walk humbly with your God?" (Micah 6:8). To me, walking humbly with God means I put my hand over my mouth as Job did and become still.

Agreeing with Paul, who said that we do not know how to pray, we dare to immerse ourselves in the silence of God's loving presence. His joyful, peaceful, gentle, kind, longsuffering, patient ways gradually rub off on us, and they become our ways. As we open our hearts to him, he fills them with his love. And his love in us will transform us just as a log, placed in a blazing fire, is transformed when it becomes totally fire.

176

The author of *The Cloud* gives us a colorful description of that transformation:

> Your whole personality will be transformed, your countenance will radiate inner beauty. . . . Your words will be few, but so fruitful and *full of fire* that the little you say will hold a world of wisdom. . . . Your silence will be peaceful, your speech helpful, and your prayer secret in the depths of your being . . . your way with others gentle, and your laughter merry, as you take delight in everything with the joy of a child.[3]

Filled with the love of God, we will be so passionately involved in life that the small flame of love within us will become a fire and we will be aglow, aflame with that love. I know that it's probably not politically correct in our civilized, sophisticated twenty-first-century world to talk about passion in our religious lives. The passion of Christ and the pain and suffering the Savior endured to redeem us are quickly passed over in our good and busy lives. In the name of tolerance, we've sanitized the chaos caused by sin—whether it is the "big" sins that destroy lives and tear families apart or the "little" sins that simply debilitate or defame character and destroy hope. We love to be scandalized by the latest gossip, but at the same time we're embarrassed to even consider a God who cares passionately for his creation.

The flame and passion of God's love burn ever brightly yet don't consume the object of his love; rather, the flame enlightens, purifies, and warms. We can draw close to God, and he will draw close to us. We can come boldly to God, or we can come cautiously and tentatively. Either way, God will respond to us with great tenderness and gentleness. God calls us to love—to love him first and then to love our world. Scripture tells us that there are many things, including knowledge, that will fail or pass away, but love is not one of them. Throughout this book I have encouraged you to join with me in slipping away from your hectic life and take time to give yourself as a gift to your Creator. Most of us have been far too involved with reading, thinking, talking, and knowing to even imagine that there might be more to loving God than engaging in all these activities or to consider silence and *unknowing* as valid forms of worship.

After reading this book, some of you may have caught a sense of a fire within that could easily become a burning flame. The fire, the longing, the desire, the love are there, deep within your spirit. They just need a little fanning, a little encouragement, to burn brighter. Then we will be able to say with St. John of the Cross: "How delicately I'm caught afire with love!"[4]

We were created to love and be loved and to live in intimate union with our loving Creator. The fruit of our love relationship with the Lord creates invisible ripples that affect the world in ways we cannot see or comprehend. By loving God wholeheartedly, we are loving his world.

You may ask, "What does being quiet in God's presence lead to? What happens after I've established an intimate relationship with the Lord and am inflamed with his love?"

The answer is twofold. On the one hand, if we are called to do so, we pass it on to others whom the Lord brings across our path. On the other hand, this intimate love relationship is an end in itself, and even if we don't pass it on overtly through words or works, when one of us in the Body of Christ moves closer to God, we all move closer to God, because we are connected.

What did Jesus say about loving God wholeheartedly? He said, "This is the first and greatest commandment.

178

And," he said, "the second is like it" (Matt. 22:38–39 NIV). We fulfill the second commandment as well when we come to God in the prayer of silence—because in our interior and spiritual being with God, we bring all our loved ones and all our world with us as we give ourselves totally to him in love. Contemplative prayer is a *faith* practice—a mystery that we cannot grasp unless we dare to *be* in the Lord's presence instead of compulsively *do*ing things. It is loving people by loving God directly, since we are all interconnected in God.

Thomas Merton said that we would be surprised if we knew how few people are holding the world together. Perhaps most of those "few" are the silent ones, the ones who participate in the life of God by loving him for himself and by giving themselves as a gift to him without words. Ecologically, we have found that what we do in one part of our planet has an effect in another part. Maybe there is more truth than we know in the words of the poet Francis Thompson when he says:

> All things by immortal
>   power
> Near or far, hiddenly,
> To each other linked are,
>   so that
> Thou canst not stir
>   a flower
> Without troubling a star.[5]

We give ourselves to God in faith, and in faith we leave the work to him. Out of our intimate love relationship—our contemplative life—will come our activity. For it is from the depths of our passion for the Lord that the burning desire comes—to do and to be whatever he calls us to. Aflame with the fire of our love of Jesus, we come out of our time of silence, out of being quiet in God's presence, to share what has radically changed us. Whether we are called to speak or to be silent, to work or to wait, to rejoice or to mourn, we show, by our very being, the way for the wounded, the lame, the crippled, the blind, and the brokenhearted to be reconciled to the Lover of their souls. The words of St. Francis of Assisi speak eloquently to us today: "Preach the Gospel always. If necessary, use words!"[6]

Remember that Jesus told the disciples: "By this will all know that you are my disciples, if you have love for one another" (John 13:35 NOAB). This is the hallmark of those who know God loves them. They will be known by their love, their gentleness, their compassion, not by their words or their knowledge. After beholding the Lord in the prayer of silence, after being held in his loving embrace, after he has healed our wounded souls, we will find ourselves living our days with joy and treating others with warmth and compassion. We will love—because he first loved us!

Give yourself the time to be alone with your Beloved; let him transform you in the light of his presence; let the fire of his love burn brightly in your heart; and then go out into the world and be amazed at what opportunities for blessing he has in store for you. As soon as you do this, you will find that God has gone before you, as the One who heals and reconciles.

If we've been called to teach and actively share this prayer, then, like the Olympic torchbearer, we run with it until we find another one who has been called to share it, and we pass it on. And that is one of the reasons for this book. Maybe your heart has been touched. Maybe you've caught a glimpse of the God who loves you passionately and unconditionally, and you are now aware that living a life that is closer to the Lord is possible. Perhaps the longing within you for something more has been awakened, and the realization that you could catch on fire with the passion of God's love thrills your soul!

If your heart has been touched, then I invite you to immerse yourself in the cloud of unknowing that is God. Ask him to increase your awareness till the small flame of his life and love kindled in you becomes a roaring fire—till you become truly aflame with love—and the warm glow of that love lights up your world! Once you feel the warmth of that fire, you won't want to give it up. You'll find you can't live without an intimate relationship with your Beloved! No one will have to tell you, cajole you, or encourage you to live in the heart of this reality. You'll recognize this place as the reason for being, and you'll rush into the arms of your Beloved.

Remember, the Lord is drawing you closer to himself. He can't bear to let you go on living so far from him!

Can you not see him waiting for you?[7]

Epilogue

My heart beat faster as I took the phone from my brother's hand. "Your sister-in-law," he had said, with a funny smile that immediately made me wonder. His wife was sitting opposite me at the kitchen table, and as I looked at her, I thought, *You're my only sister-in-law!*

"Hello," I said tentatively into the phone.

"Hello, darling," came straight back to me in a cheery familiar voice from the past. It *was* my sister-in-law! Lesley! My late husband's eldest sister! Twenty-four years had passed since I last heard her voice.

A few hours later, on that lovely Australian spring day in November, I was to meet Lesley, as well as my niece, Suzanne, and Sue's teenage son, Bradley, both of whom lived only twenty minutes away from my brother's house. Within a few weeks I was reunited with and welcomed by my parents-in-law, and another sister, Ellen, and her family. I was stunned by the love expressed and by the acceptance. I was amazed that they were willing to open themselves up to the painful memories that my presence inevitably aroused.

In 1965, when my beloved husband Raymond died beside me in a road accident, I had wanted to die too. Both families, his and mine, were heartbroken. He had

183

been a joyful, loving, vibrant light in all of our lives, and his loss was very painful. After this tragedy we all had struggled with believing in a God of love.

Seeking relief from my pain, I moved out of state and eventually out of the country, gradually losing contact with all of my husband's family. During the past year, they had come to mind many times. I had looked in the Melbourne phone book in vain. The whole family had moved. My last resort was an acquaintance in Lesley's old neighborhood. Several months earlier, before arriving in Australia for Christmas, I had sent a message to this friend that I'd like to get back in touch with my in-laws, and then I had put it from my mind.

Just walking into that family rolled the years back, putting us all face-to-face with the raw, unhealed wounds of the past. The unconditional acceptance and joy with which I was received surprised and overwhelmed me, giving me the sense of being the returning prodigal. Facing the pain and joy of reconciliation spread a healing mantle over all of us, bringing peace at last.

The whole experience was made possible, as far as I was concerned, because of the monumental changes that had been taking place in my relationship with the Lord.

I know that my reconciliation with my husband's family was no accident. The timing for them and for me was just right. Their running and embracing and kissing me (see Luke 15:20 JB) was evidence of our mutual longing, of being ready to accept healing, and of a loving God who desires reconciliation for all of his creation.

The first day I visited with my parents-in-law in early December, we began by sitting around the kitchen table, drinking tea, and catching up on our lost twenty-four years. Then Mum took me out onto the veranda, pointed to a very small, lushly foliaged camellia bush growing beside the steps, and said, "Do you remember what you gave me on the Mother's Day before Raymond died? You gave me a camellia bush. And that's it."

I looked closely at the little bush. It was about nine inches high, but underneath the lush new growth was a thick, wizened strangely twisted trunk.

My mother-in-law laughed and then continued. "That bush has almost died a dozen times. For twenty-four years I have struggled to keep it alive, and it has never done any good—until this year. Earlier this year it began to grow. In July, for the first time, it was completely covered in red flowers. Look at it now. It's strong and healthy at last."

As I looked at the scarred old trunk of the camellia bush and at the new growth, I knew that the years of extreme pain, grief, and mourning were over for us all.

The following May, shortly after Mother's Day (which falls in late autumn in Australia), I had a note from my mother-in-law. "When I came out of the house on Mother's Day morning, I was surprised to be greeted by one lone flower on the camellia bush. I picked it and put it in the vase beside Raymond's photo. The bush continues to grow. It has grown a foot since you were here. I know that the unseasonable flower on Mother's Day is a message from God to remind me that he loves me."

In July—late winter in Australia, the usual time for camellia flowers—she wrote again to say that the bush was totally covered in blooms, as it had been the previous year. The next May, on Mother's Day morning, once again a single flower brightened my mother-in-law's day.

Then, a single, unseasonable flower appeared on the camellia bush the next year on Mother's Day morning as well—making it three years in a row! Amazing! Now, whenever any of us looks at the camellia bush—which still thrives and is over seven feet tall—we are reminded that life and love are triumphant after all.

185

To me this story is a picture of the way in which our loving God's unexpected grace is poured out on us all. Our Lord is in the healing business. He longs to make us whole and complete. He encourages reconciliation, and through it, that which is broken becomes whole. I know that God, through his gracious acceptance of our frail humanity, longs to fill all of our lives with loving surprises. He can't wait for the flow of his love to heal us of our deep wounds. He wants his children to love and appreciate each other, because he sees each of us as precious.

And precious we are.

Notes

Introduction

1. Some teachers of the prayer of silence call it meditation, and some contemplation. I use the words as defined by F. L. Cross, ed., in *The Oxford Dictionary of the Christian Church*, 2d ed. (New York: Oxford University Press, 1983), pp. 898, 341: *"meditation:* mental prayer in its discursive form"; *"contemplation:* non-discursive mental prayer, as distinguished from meditation."

2. William Johnston, ed., *The Cloud of Unknowing* and *The Book of Privy Counseling* (New York: Bantam Doubleday Dell, 1973), chap. 4, pp. 53, 50; emphasis mine.

3. Ibid., chap. 2, p. 76; emphasis mine.

4. Ibid., chap. 5, p. 53.

5. Ibid., chap. 4, p. 53; emphasis mine.

6. Ibid., chap. 3, p. 49; emphasis mine.

7. Ibid., chap. 4, p. 50.

8. Ibid., chap. 7, p. 56.

9. Ibid., chap. 1, p. 46.

Part 1 Why Be . . . Quiet in His Presence?

Epigraph from Macrina Wiederkehr, *A Tree Full of Angels* (San Francisco: HarperSanFrancisco, 1988), 57. Reprinted by permission of HarperCollins Publishers Inc.

Chapter 1 A Particular Love

1. Brennan Manning tape "Contemplatives in Action" (Minneapolis, MN: Church of the Open Door, 1999), #1; in my own words.

2. Nicene Creed, *The Book of Common Prayer* (New York: Seabury Press, 1979), 358.

3. Attributed to Richard of Chicester, a.d. 1197–1253; *The Hymnal* 1982, according to the use of the Episcopal Church (New York: The Church Hymnal Corporation, 1985), hymn no. 654.

Chapter 2 Drawn by Love's Longing

1. Johnston, ed., *The Cloud of Unknowing*, chap. 2, p. 46.
2. Briege O'Hare, OSC, *Taste the Hidden Sweetness: Songs of the Mystical Life* (Monasterevin, Co. Kildare, Ireland: St. Clare's Convent, 1993). From the letters of St. Clare to St. Agnes of Prague, Clare Centenary 1193–1993, "Before I Say Farewell," p. 7; used by permission.
3. Johnston, ed., *The Cloud of Unknowing*, chap. 5, p. 53.
4. Ibid., chap. 12, p. 63.
5. Ibid., chap. 4, p. 50.

Chapter 3 Made for Love

1. Frank Sheed, trans., *The Confessions of St. Augustine* (New York: Sheed and Ward, 1943), 1.

Chapter 5 I Will Never Forsake You

1. Johnston, ed., *The Cloud of Unknowing*, chap. 6, p. 84.

Part 2 How to Be . . . Quiet in His Presence

Epigraph from Henri J. M. Nouwen, *The Road to Daybreak: A Spiritual Journey* (New York: Doubleday, 1988), 29. Used by permission.

Chapter 6 Steps to Being Quiet in His Presence

1. Sofia Cavalletti, *The Religious Potential of the Child* (Ramsey, N.J.: Paulist Press, 1983), 174.
2. M. Basil Pennington, *Centering Prayer* (New York: Doubleday, 1980), 65.
3. Johnston, ed., *The Cloud of Unknowing*, chap. 3, p. 154.
4. Some churches have contemplative prayer groups that meet on a regular basis. To find one in your area, or to attend a retreat that focuses on the prayer of silence, contact your local churches, check their web pages, or look up the following web sites: http://www.st-francis-lutheran.org; http://www.unionlife.com; http://www.centeringprayer.com. Centering prayer sometimes brings to the surface troubling memories or feelings. If this happens, it is a good idea to have a spiritual companion or spiritual director to turn to. Your local churches may be able to help you find one. A resource for spiritual directon is: http://www.sdiworld.org.

Chapter 7 Resting in God

1. Brennan Manning tape, "Healing the Image of God in Ourselves." Session 3.
2. Reflecting on the Scriptures: also called *Lectio Divina,* or Divine Reading. See *Too Deep for Words* by Thelma Hall (Mahwah, N.J.: Paulist Press, 1988). See also http://www.lectiodivina.org.

Chapter 8 Becoming like a Little Child

1. Johnston, ed., *The Cloud of Unknowing*, chap. 17, p. 71.
2. Margaret Montreuil, Minneapolis, Minn., personal e-mail to author, May 2001.

Chapter 11 Opening the Door

1. Clifton Wolters, trans., *The Cloud of Unknowing and Other Works* (London: Penguin, 1978), chap. 26, p. 94.
2. In F. L. Cross, ed., *The Oxford Dictionary of the Christian Church*, 2d ed. (New York: Oxford University Press, 1983), 1472.
3. Rev. David Watson, in a sermon at St. Michael-le-Belfrey, York, England, c. 1978.
4. Johnston, ed., *The Cloud of Unknowing*, chap. 13, p. 172.

Chapter 12 Do Not Be Afraid . . . You Are Mine

1. Alfred, Lord Tennyson, "The Higher Pantheism," in *The Works of Tennyson* (New York: Macmillan, 1931).

Chapter 13 Like a Weaned Child

1. Tennyson, "The Higher Pantheism."
2. Early (third and fourth centuries) references to Christians going out into the desert to be alone with God have encouraged subsequent generations to seek him in silence. Monastic communities generally encouraged contemplatives, but after the dissolution of the monasteries following the Reformation, Protestants avoided monastic practices to focus, instead, on Bible study and spontaneous discursive prayer; fearful Counter-Reformation Catholics also moved away from traditional monasticism to focus almost exclusively on the Daily Offices, discursive meditation, and written prayers. In the twentieth century, several people living in monastic communities in different parts of the world revived the practice of contemplative prayer and began to teach it to religious and lay persons, both Catholic and Protestant. There are now many groups around the world dedicated to the teaching and encouragment of this practice. See http://www.st-francis-lutheran.org; http://www.wccm.org (World Community for Christian Meditation); and http://www.centeringprayer.com (Contemplative Outreach).
3. Madeleine L'Engle, "After Annunciation," in *The Irrational Season* (New York: Seabury Press, 1977), 27. Reprinted by permission of HarperCollins Publishers Inc.

Chapter 14 Gazing on the Lord

1. Helen H. Lemmel, "Turn Your Eyes upon Jesus," in *Worship and Service Hymnal* (Chicago: Hope Publishing, 1957), no. 220.
2. St. John of the Cross, "The Spiritual Canticle," in *The Poems of St. John of the Cross*, trans. John Frederick Nims (New York: Grove Press, 1959), 111.

3. Quietly playing some beautiful music or a worship song as we begin our time of sitting with God is very helpful. I have created my own Prayer Timers: I taped a favorite song and followed it immediately with 20 minutes of silence which ends with a bar of music to indicate that the time is up. I also have 10- and 15-minute timers. Prayer Timers such as these may be purchased from www.unionlife.com. Also see www.centeringprayer.com.

4. O'Hare, *Taste the Hidden Sweetness: Songs of the Mystical Life,* "Gaze Upon the Lord," 5. Used by permission.

Part 3 How Being Quiet in His Presence Changes Your Life

Epigraph from George A. Maloney, *Inscape* and *The Breath of the Mystic* (Denville, N.J.: Dimension Books, 1974), 168, 42.

Chapter 15 No Measuring Stick

1. Johnston, ed., *The Cloud of Unknowing,* chap. 28, p. 85.
2. Ibid., chap. 7, p. 56.
3. Michael Molinos, *The Spiritual Guide,* trans. JoAnne Chappell (Sargent, Ga.: SeedSowers, 1992), 48.

Chapter 16 Being the Beloved

1. William Johnston, *The Inner Eye of Love* (San Francisco: Harper and Row, 1978), 95.
2. St. John of the Cross, "The Living Flame of Love," in *The Poems of St. John of the Cross,* 23.

Chapter 17 Letting Go

1. Sheed, trans., *The Confessions of St. Augustine,* 1.

Chapter 18 The Cloud of Forgetting

1. Johnston, ed., *The Cloud of Unknowing,* chap. 26, p. 83.
2. Ibid., chap. 5, p. 53, emphasis mine.
3. Macrina Wiederkehr, "A Prayer to Own Your Beauty," in *Seasons of Your Heart: Prayers and Reflections* (San Francisco: HarperSanFrancisco, 1991), 71; emphasis mine. Reprinted by permission.

Chapter 19 Aflame with Love

1. Johnston, ed., *The Cloud of Unknowing,* chap. 22, p. 186.
2. Ibid., chap. 7, p. 56, emphasis mine.
3. Ibid., chap. 19, pp. 182–83.
4. St. John of the Cross, "The Living Flame of Love," 23.
5. Francis Thompson, "The Mistress of Vision," in *The Works of Francis Thompson, Poems,* vol. 2, ed. Wilfrid Meynell (New York: Charles Scribner, 1913).
6. Francis of Assisi, source unknown.
7. Wolters, trans., *The Cloud of Unknowing,* chap. 26, p. 94.

Bibliography

In addition to books cited in Notes:

Bakke, Jeannette A. *Holy Invitations: Exploring Spiritual Direction*. Grand Rapids: Baker, 2000.

Benson, Robert. *Living Prayer*. New York: Putnam, 1999.

Buechner, Frederick. *Telling the Truth: The Gospel as Tragedy, Comedy and Fairy Tale*. New York: Harper & Row, 1977.

Casey, Michael. *Towards God: The Western Tradition of Contemplation*. Melbourne, Australia: Collins Dove, 1989.

Clark, John, trans. *Story of a Soul: The Autobiography of St. Therese of Lisieux*. Washington, D.C.: ICS Publications, 1972.

De Mello, Anthony. *Awareness: The Perils and Opportunities of Reality*. New York: Doubleday, 1990.

Finley, James. *The Awakening Call: Fostering Intimacy with God*. Notre Dame, Ind.: Ave Maria Press, 1984.

French, R. M., trans. *The Way of the Pilgrim*. New York: Ballantine Books, 1974.

Frost, Bede. *Saint John of the Cross*. New York: Harper & Brothers, 1937.

Guyon, Jeanne. *Experiencing the Depths of Jesus Christ*. Gardiner, Maine: Christian Books, 1975.

Johnson, Jan. *When the Soul Listens: Finding Rest and Direction in Contemplative Prayer*. Colorado Springs: NavPress, 1999.

Johnston, William. *Being in Love: The Practice of Christian Prayer*. London: Fount/Harper Collins Religious, 1988.

Keating, Thomas. *Open Mind, Open Heart: The Contemplative Dimension of the Gospel*. New York: Continuum, 1986.

Main, John. *Letters from the Heart: Christian Monasticism and the Renewal of Community*. New York: Crossroad, 1982.

Maloney, George A. *Inward Stillness*. Denville, N.J.: Dimension, 1976.

Manning, Brennan. *Abba's Child: The Cry of the Heart for Intimate Belonging*. Colorado Springs: NavPress, 1994.

Mason, Mike. *The Mystery of Marriage: Meditations on the Miracle*. Sisters, Ore.: Multnomah, 1985.

McNamara, William. *Mystical Passion: The Art of Christian Loving*. Rockport, Mass.: Element, 1977.

Merton, Thomas. *New Seeds of Contemplation*. New York: New Directions, 1961.

Nouwen, Henri J. M. *Clowning in Rome: Reflections on Solitude, Celibacy, Prayer, and Contemplation*. New York: Doubleday, 1979.

Rolheiser, Ronald. *The Holy Longing: The Search for a Christian Spirituality*. New York: Doubleday, 1999.

Shannon, William. *Silence on Fire: The Prayer of Awareness*. New York: Crossroad, 1991.

Smith, Martin L. *Reconciliation: Preparing for Confession in the Episcopal Church*. Cambridge, Mass.: Cowley, 1985.

Steere, Douglas V. *Together in Solitude*. New York: Crossroad, 1982.

Talbot, John Michael. *The Lover and the Beloved: A Way of Franciscan Prayer*. New York: Crossroad, 1988.

Taylor, Brian C. *Becoming Christ: Transformation through Contemplation*. Cambridge, Mass.: Cowley, 2002.

Van Breemen, Peter G. *As Bread That is Broken*. Denville, N.J.: Dimension, 1974.

Volkman, Bill. *Basking in His Presence: A Call to the Prayer of Silence*. Glen Ellyn, Ill.: Union Life, 1986.

Walsh, Kilian, trans. *Bernard of Clairvaux*, vol. 2, *On the Song of Songs*. Kalamazoo, Mich.: Cistercian Publications, 1981.

Jan Harris was executive editor of the print edition of *Union Life* magazine for eighteen years. She leads contemplative prayer retreats in the United States, Canada, and Australia and has written several articles on the contemplative life. You may contact her at:

P. O. Box 2877
Glen Ellyn, IL 60138
e-mail: jan@unionlife.com